THE ETF INVESTOR

HOW TO INVEST IN EXCHANGE-TRADED FUNDS

JEFF LUKE

DISCLAIMER

The material in this book is for informational purposes only. Nothing in this book constitutes an offer or solicitation of financial advice and is not intended to provide investment, legal, tax, or other professional or financial advice.

Nothing in this book is to be construed as an offer or a recommendation to buy or sell a security. Additionally, the material in this book does not constitute a representation that the investments described herein are suitable or appropriate for any person.

Such content therefore should not be relied upon for the making of any personal financial and investment decisions. Persons accessing this information are strongly encouraged to obtain appropriate professional advice before making any investment or financial decision.

Before investing, please follow these simple guidelines:

1. Never invest in something that you don't understand.
2. Never invest based on anyone else's opinion.
3. Ask for assistance if you need it.

DEDICATION

For my reader

"Imagination is more important than knowledge. Knowledge is limited. Imagination encircles the world."

— Einstein

CONTENTS

1. Hero in Brazil — 1
2. What is an ETF? — 3
3. Investing made simple — 9
4. Set up a brokerage account — 16
5. Types of orders — 18
6. Investing at intervals — 27
7. Simplicity with one ETF — 31
8. ETFs help you keep calm — 40
9. Factor Investing — 44
10. The 25 ETFs — 49
11. Small-cap ETFs — 51
12. Small-cap Value ETFs — 63
13. Mega-Cap Growth ETF — 80
14. Mid-cap ETFs — 84
15. VanEck Vectors Morningstar Wide Moat — 93
16. O'Shares Global Internet Giants — 96
17. ARK Innovation — 100
18. WisdomTree Cloud Computing — 103
19. SPDR S&P Biotech — 107
20. iShares Nasdaq Biotechnology — 109
21. Vanguard Health Care — 112
22. Three Dividend ETFs — 114
23. Blackrock iShares Core Dividend Growth — 116
24. ProShares S&P 500 Dividend Aristocrats fund — 118
25. Global X Super Dividend Fund — 120
26. Ark Fintech Innovation — 124
27. Technology Sector ETFs — 128
28. International ETFs — 133
29. Putting it all together — 136
30. Your biggest obstacle — 139
31. Active managers choose index investing — 146
32. Improving investor behavior — 149
33. A behavior trick — 151
34. Pay yourself first — 154

35. Think About Rip Van Winkle — 160
36. Creation and redemption — 162
37. Plan for success — 171
38. How do you define success? — 174
39. Useful Resources — 176
    Thank you — 179
    Afterword — 181
    Disclosure — 184

    Connect — 185
    About the Author — 187
    Also by Jeff Luke — 189
    Notes — 191

1

HERO IN BRAZIL

I was once a hero in Brazil. One day in the operating room, Dr. Batista was in the midst of a long procedure when he asked his assistants to hand him the scalpel.

I traveled to the jungles of Brazil many years ago to photograph the famous heart surgeon, Dr. Randas Batista. He had invited me to ride horses on his ranch and photograph him doing the operation that made him famous.

Batista had been operating on a patient with an enlarged heart using a procedure he pioneered. He was about to cut a section of myocardium from the patient's left ventricle, but when he extended his hand for his scalpel his assistants remained motionless.

"*Onde está minha faca?*" he demanded, in Portuguese, "*Where is my knife?*" His eyes went from one assistant to the other, scanning their faces, waiting for the knife. The doctor's anger was palpable, and for good reason: it's dangerous to lose a sharp tool in a patient's body.

To protect against loss of instruments in Seattle, I remember scrub nurses kept a careful tally using a whiteboard and black marker. They made a mark in the "IN" column every time a tool entered the surgical field, and another in the "OUT" column when it left.

The misplaced medical device was a source of grave concern. The doctor seethed at the nurses and techs for not paying closer attention, his anger rising as a gradual build-up of lava and pressure before the eruption. We all waited for the explosion. He growled, "What the hell were you doing, out drinking all night? I don't pay you to stand around! Where the hell's my knife?" Batista is 6'5" and could have easily thrown any of them across the room and into a clean white wall. The nurses and staff stood quietly alongside the anesthetized patient, saying nothing, hoping for some miracle to calm the storm.

Suddenly, from my perch atop a chair where I'd been taking photos, I spotted the glimmering blade. "*Está no chão!*" I shouted, "*It's on the ground!*"

The scalpel had slid down a crease in the surgical drape and landed upon the ground without a sound.

I'm perceptive when it comes to noticing details around me, and that helps as a photographer. Strong skills of perception also help me focus on what matters as an investor.

While this book might not save your life, it will help you pick ETFs that make sense. This book will help you feel more confident and in control of your decisions, so when you arrive at the last page you will know much more about ETFs than you know right now.

We'll start by asking why ETFs might make sense for you, and then we'll look at the simplest way to start.

So, before we get started, what is an ETF?

2

WHAT IS AN ETF?

An exchange-traded fund (ETF) is an investment fund traded on stock exchanges, much like stocks[1]. ETFs provide a simple, low-cost, tax-efficient way to invest in stocks, bonds, or commodities in one simple package.

ETFs offer investors a way to pool their money in a fund that makes investments in stocks, bonds, or other assets in exchange for an interest in that investment pool. There is one main difference: you buy or sell mutual fund shares from the pool at a price calculated at the *end* of the trading day, but you trade ETFs on a stock exchange *during* the trading day at fluctuating market prices[2].

Things to Consider before Investing in ETFs

ETFs hold a variety of assets just like mutual funds, but they're not mutual funds. ETFs combine features of a mutual fund, which can be purchased or redeemed at the end of each trading day with the features of a stock, whose shares trade throughout the day at market prices.

Unlike with mutual fund shares, retail investors can only buy and sell ETF shares in market transactions. So, as an ETF investor, you will need to learn how to trade shares on a stock exchange. Mutual fund investors do not use a stock exchange because they buy or sell shares from an investment "pool," without interacting directly with the market[3].

You will learn much more about the "secret sauce" that makes this all happen behind the scenes in Chapter 31, "Creation and Redemption."

You know more than you think

If you're reading this book you probably know something about how the stock market works. Maybe you've owned mutual funds, or you have heard about the S&P 500.

So, if I asked you, "Do you know what the S&P 500 is?" you might say, "It's the largest 500 stocks in the US," and you'd be right.

When you want to invest, you can either research which one of those stocks to buy, or you can pay a professional fund manager to go buy them for you.

But, wouldn't it be easier if you could trade all those stocks at once, in one easy package? What if you could just make one trade for $100 and buy all the stocks in the S&P? That is what an ETF lets you do. It's a wrapper that you put around a bunch of stocks so you can buy or sell the whole basket at once.

Some ETFs hold 40 stocks, and some more than 4,000. In this book, we'll talk about many different kinds of ETFs, and you'll soon see which ones make sense for you depending on where you are in your investing journey.

Types of ETFs

- **Index-Based ETFs** are the most commonly traded ETFs in the marketplace. These ETFs seek to track a securities index like the S&P 500 stock index and generally invest primarily in the component securities of the index. For

example, the Vanguard S&P 500 ETF, which seeks to track the S&P 500 stock index, invests in most or all of the equity securities contained in the S&P 500 stock index. Some, but not all, ETFs may post their holdings on their websites daily.
- **Actively managed ETFs** are not based on an index. Instead, they seek to achieve a stated investment objective by investing in a portfolio of stocks, bonds, and other assets. For example, Ark Fintech Innovation is an actively managed ETF that invests in domestic and foreign stocks of companies that are engaged in the Fund's investment theme of financial technology ("Fintech") innovation. Unlike an index-based ETF, an adviser of an actively managed ETF may actively buy or sell stocks in the portfolio without having to conform with an index[4].

ETFs are like zoo animals

Think of all the animals you might find in a zoo. You can make one long list of animals from aardvark to zebra. If all of those animals were an ETF you could call it ZOO, or you could put the animals in smaller groups based on distinct characteristics. This is the same idea as putting stocks into groups so you can trade them as ETFs.

JEFF LUKE

You can put animals into one big group or smaller groups based on unique characteristics. Similarly, ETFs let you put stocks into different groups. Artwork by Edwin Yaguar Chávez.

Let's put animals into groups and give them symbols as though they were ETFs.

- ZOO - All animals
- APE - Chimpanzees, gorillas, macaques
- BEAR - Pandas, koalas, polar bears
- BIRD - Parrots, peacocks, hummingbirds
- CATS - Lions, tigers, leopards
- ELE - African, Asian, and Indian elephants
- REP - Snakes, iguanas, chameleons

So, if you want to invest in all animals you could buy ZOO, and if you only want bears you could pick BEAR and get koalas, polar bears, grizzlies, pandas, etc.

There are many stocks available to group into ETFs, just as there are many animals at the zoo. When you set out to select ETFs as your investments your task is to decide if you want to buy all of the stocks available or if you prefer to buy a smaller group, or subset, of all the stocks in the market.

Ticker symbols for ETFs are those unique combinations of letters like the ones used for animals above. These unique three or four-letter codes will help you find more information about each ETF when you're researching them, and it will help you identify the ETF on your brokerage platform if and when you decide to invest.

Useful ETF facts

1. You can invest in ETFs for the price of one share. Most brokerage firms provide commission-free trades.
2. Most ETF providers charge investors an annual fee called an expense ratio, which is expressed as a percent of the money you invest in the ETF. This ratio is listed next to each ETF profiled in this book.
3. In general, index-based ETFs have lower expense ratios, and actively managed ETFs have higher expense ratios.

I'll be your guide on this adventure as we explore many ETFs that I think you will find useful. There are thousands of ETFs available to trade, and while it's not practical to cover them all in one book, I will point out what I believe are the most important factors to consider.

There are many ETF providers: Ark Investments, Blackrock (iShares), Fidelity, Invesco, Charles Schwab, State Street (SPDRs), Vanguard, WisdomTree, and hundreds of others.

These providers offer ETFs that invest in different geographic areas, in companies of a specific size, in sectors of the economy, or according to investment themes.

Here is a list of several Vanguard sector ETFs to give you an idea of how ETFs organize stocks into groups so investors can trade them.

- VTI - all US companies
- VOO - largest US companies
- VO - mid-cap
- VCR - consumer discretionary
- VDC - consumer staples
- VWO - emerging markets
- VDE - energy
- VFH - financial
- VHT - health care
- VYM - high dividend yield
- VNQ - real estate
- VB - small-cap
- VGT - technology

While Vanguard offers an array of low-cost ETFs, many other providers have found creative ways to package stocks into innovative ETFs. It's worth taking a close look at a variety of offerings available before you trade.

As we explore the investment landscape you may instantly recognize some funds, like those that invest in the S&P 500. You'll also discover that some ETFs focus on niches like biotech, cloud computing, fintech, health care, Internet, or high dividend yield stocks.

No matter what kind of stocks you want to trade — the whole stock market or just a section of it — ETFs let you trade a group of stocks in one easy package.

3

INVESTING MADE SIMPLE

I was once where you are today. I knew little about ETFs but was curious and wanted to learn about them. One year ago I had not yet invested in them.

You may wonder why I stayed away, and I offer you a simple reason: you could buy index funds free of charge. ETFs trade like stocks which means every time you traded you had to pay an online broker a $7 or $10 commission.

Of course, all of that changed when a price war among brokers drove trade costs to zero.[1] That meant *you could buy and sell ETFs free of charge.* That was a game-changer because, with those frictional trading fees out of the way, it was an easy decision to invest with ETFs.

So, while I didn't have experience trading ETFs a year ago, I had a great deal of experience as a mutual fund and stock investor. Because I know how much time and energy go into researching stocks and picking "just the right one" I could instantly identify the benefits that ETFs provide: broad exposure to an asset class at low cost and instant diversification.

I have a "beginner's mind" when it comes to ETFs.[2] I'm sharing what I've learned with you through a lot of reading and aggregating data about ETFs. I want to tell you about what I've discovered as I would with a friend.

It was a stroke of luck that this book came to fruition. I was deep into writing a book about index funds, which are similar to ETFs in many ways, but lack specific cost-savings and tax efficiencies that are unique to ETFs.[3]

In January of 2020, I remember telling a writer friend, Jonathan Butz, that I was writing a book about index funds. "Why the hell would you do that?" he asked. "You should write a book about ETFs!"

I was surprised, yet impressed by his directive. Some people might not care about your project and encourage you to just keep on doing whatever you're doing. But Jon felt that ETFs are newer and better than index funds, and he wanted me to write a more relevant book.

Keep in mind that a year ago *I had never invested with ETFs*. That should give you a ton of confidence because if a photographer with no prior experience investing in ETFs can invest with them, you can too.

I was just starting research for this book when the pandemic caused havoc on society, jobs, and the stock market. Markets dropped suddenly each day for about a week, the Dow dropping 500 points one day and 700 the next. Suddenly the drops became extreme, with the Dow losing 1000 points in a day. People were fearful about their health, their jobs, and their investments. The basics of life, everything from toilet paper to disinfectant was flying off the shelves, and this irrational panic was reflected in plummeting stock prices.

Stocks got cheap because people were uncertain about the future: whether humans would survive, go to work, travel in planes and cruise ships, stay at hotels, eat at restaurants, and shop in malls. *Everything* we did suddenly changed, and investors ditched thousands of stocks of companies they thought might go out of business or, if they survived, take years to recover.

Amid the chaos and stress I knew it was time to buy. You make money in markets when you bet the other way, and since people were scared and prices were cheap, I knew it was time to be brave. When everyone was losing their minds it was time to use mine to implement the simple ETF strategy I describe in this book.

ETFs made investing simple

I needed a simple way to invest in the market that I could do right away without having to think too much. I knew that if started trying to pick the perfect stocks it would take too long to decide. I could not delay the decision. ETFs turned out to be the perfect solution.

I'm not a typical investor in that I don't get spooked by falling markets. It's like I got a vaccine against fear and these things don't affect me, and I know I'm lucky in that respect. Maybe as a 26-year-old investor I might have been concerned, but thinking back, I was courageous then too. I was five years into investing when the Dotcom bust hit, and I didn't sell anything. So, I must have immunity to market panic and though I feel the panic that others feel, I don't act on it. I wait for my chance to buy when everyone else is selling.

This bravery creates wealth. Most people would rather buy stocks when everything is smooth sailing and they've been going up for a while, which is why *most people are not good investors*. Instead, people should want to buy when everyone around them is talking about how the market may never recover from the pandemic.

I'm aware that many readers might not share this calm in the middle of a storm. I know many people who have invested for years and *still get scared* when the market drops. It's human nature to act based on emotional reactions to perceived loss.

Keep in mind that *I feel those same emotions*, like a poker player who feels strong excitement (or disgust) in the middle of a hand when there's a lot of money in the pot. They can't let their emotions give away their hand, so despite a million thoughts in their head they have to display the outward calm of a cliff diver if they want to make it out of the hand alive.

By the same token, even if I wake up in the morning to see the Dow down 1,400 points I couldn't run like a scalded rabbit.

Just to give you an idea of the high level of fear in the stock market, many investors sold stocks out of fear. Others wondered if it might make sense to get out of the market while it kept falling, thinking that it might make sense to buy back in after the smoke had cleared.[4] I was at dinner with friends, and one of them said he was going to wait around until after the market reached bottom, and *then he'd buy back in*. That's easy to say, but not easy to do.

Nobody knew how bad things would get, and nobody knew when the bloodshed would end. Even if the United States and financial markets recovered, nobody knew if it would take a year, or three, or even 10. The fear of losing money in stocks and having to wait many years caused panic selling.

One YouTuber I followed at the time recorded a video titled "I Sold All My Stocks" and listed all of the reasons the stock market was in deep doo-doo.[5] Let me remind readers that we now know that a vaccine was developed and progress made against Covid-19, back in March, April, and May 2020, many famous investors either stoked fear among investors by saying things would get worse, as Bill Ackman did,[6] or sold billions of dollars in stocks because of the uncertain future for air travel, as Buffett did when he sold all of Berkshire Hathaway's airline stocks.[7] The selling — whether it was done for profit or because of panic — caused the market to tank because of fast-spreading fear about humanity's future.

ETFs let you buy many stocks at once

While the world was burning down around me, I decided to buy stocks. The problem is I didn't know *which stocks to buy*. Also, things were happening so fast in the stock market I didn't have time to think. I needed to make a good decision quickly. ETFs came to the rescue because they let me buy many stocks — a whole group — in one simple investment.

Crushed it with two ETFs during the crash

So, what did I do? Well, I had a chunk of money set aside to invest, and I was determined to put it into ETFs because I was writing a book about them, and it's kind of an unwritten rule that you should have experience in the thing you're writing about. I have 20 years of experience investing in index funds, which are like the cousins of ETFs. So I know a ton about what they hold and how you can buy a whole universe of stocks in one easy purchase.

This was crucial because as the stock market was tanking, with the Dow down 1,000 or more points a day several times a week, I could not stop and think about which individual stocks to buy. Everything was coming apart at the seams as panic gripped the stock market. People were all running for the exits of this burning building. Even Warren Buffett was fleeing his whole collection of airline stocks.

With one Vanguard S&P 500 ETF purchase, I instantly owned a slice of Apple, Microsoft, Amazon, Facebook, Alphabet, Berkshire Hathaway, Visa, JP Morgan, Johnson & Johnson, and Walmart, and hundreds of other companies.[8]

I also invested in the Vanguard Small-Cap ETF (VB) which holds 1442 different companies. So, if you add up those stocks with the 500 large companies in the S&P 500 ETF, you can see those two ETF investments made me part owner of 1,942 different companies.[9]

ETFs made it easy to act decisively at a crucial time. With markets falling quickly, it would be easy to get stuck in "analysis paralysis" and put off the decision by not doing anything. You put it off for a few days, and then a few weeks, and before you know it, markets recovered and you never did anything because you were sucking your thumb waiting for the right time to make a decision…and that moment never arrived.

Had I tried picking stocks *I might have bought nothing*. I could still be sitting on my hands and waiting. Do you know what happened while other "investors" were waiting for a bell to ring signifying a bottom had been reached? The market bounced sharply upward, continued its climb, and never looked back! March 23rd was the lowest point in the Corona Crash,[10] yet the day came and went without fanfare.

Only the lucky ones bought all their stocks on that one day. I didn't know a perfect time to buy, but I invested early and at intervals because I wanted take advantage of the fear and the concomitant low prices. I had no idea that the stock market would recover in March and the valuable lesson others can learn is to invest when prices are cheap, because you don't know how long they will stay that way. The market began its recovery from the Corona Crash one month after it started, and kept climbing up.

It seems as though *many people thought they would have more time* to buy stocks when they were cheap. I also believed that I would have several months to buy (because during earlier crashes like the Dotcom crash, and the financial crisis there were months to buy before stocks recovered. Still, I had no crystal ball, so I just started investing when the market began to fall fast.

If I thought too much about it and tried to make a list of individual stocks to buy, this quest for the perfect stock would have caused me to miss an excellent opportunity.

When I look at the screenshots of my first ever ETF trades (you'll see them in Chapter 6) you will see that they document how to place trades. I didn't make a big deal about the good timing of those purchases because they were kind of lucky. I didn't know when the market would recover, and I just hoped it would.

Yes, the timing of those two ETF investments was opportune, but the message I'd like you to take away is that ETFs enabled me to act decisively and capture a wide universe of stocks with a couple of simple investments.

Three things you should know:

1. ETFs greatly simplify investing
2. One or two ETFs provide instant diversification
3. You don't need perfect timing

Later in life, when you look back on your investing career, any few months will be just a blip on the chart. The stock market dip during the spring of 2020 will be lost in all the ups and downs of a 10 or 20-year chart.

However, *the fact that you invested* at intervals over a long period will have a meaningful impact on your investing results. You must realize that you don't have to maximize every opportunity. Maximizing your returns by making a few well-timed investments is not as effective as investing through thick and thin — especially through thin.

After years of investing you will see that month-to-month consistency wins. You just want to be *in the market* if you intend to compound your money for a long period. Your enemy is your own tendency to cash out at the wrong time based on emotions.

ETFs compound dollars over time

It doesn't matter if the market is going up or down, or if stocks have dropped a lot recently or there's smooth sailing: if you want to compound your investing dollars over time, history shows you will be better off in stocks than cash, money markets, or bonds. ETFs let you harness the stock market's return in a low-expense and tax-efficient way.

Whether you're planning on growing your money for the long-term to make a future purchase, or to accumulate assets for retirement, ETFs can make sense in your portfolio.

4

SET UP A BROKERAGE ACCOUNT

If you want to trade ETFs you will need to set up a brokerage account. It's easier than you think to set one up, and you can do it from a laptop or your phone. You will need to choose a brokerage firm like E*Trade, Fidelity, Robinhood, Schwab, TD Ameritrade, Vanguard, or any other brokerage firm you choose.

The brokerage account application takes about 10 minutes to complete, and once you fill it out you may wait three to five days for confirmation that your account has been established. Once complete you can transfer funds into the brokerage account from your linked bank account.

Once your brokerage account is funded you can trade ETFs. I use Vanguard's mobile app because I've been a Vanguard customer for years and I like their customer service, but you can trade ETFs with any brokerage firm or with an app like Robinhood.

If you already possess experience trading stocks, you will find that ETFs trade with the same order types as stocks. For readers who are new to trading, I highly recommend learning as much as you can ahead of time. You can do that through reading this book, watching videos, and reading articles online[1].

Take your time and don't feel rushed to learn everything right away. While trading ETFs yourself is easy to do, I think you'll find that it takes some time to familiarize yourself with the steps until you gain confidence. If you have questions you can call your brokerage firm's customer service phone number with questions.

There are a few basic items you should be clear about before you place your first trade. Some people never take the time to understand order types and just start trading right away. I think it's worth taking the time to learn about order types before you trade.

So, what are the two order types you should know before you start trading ETFs?

5

TYPES OF ORDERS

There are different ways to place your order to trade ETFs, and each provides a different level of control over your trade.

When you begin the process of placing your trade you will be given a choice of "Order type" and can choose either a *market order* or *limit order*. The type of order you choose can affect the trade execution.

When you hit "enter" or "submit" to place an order through your online brokerage account – that's only the beginning of the transaction. Your broker's firm must then send your order to a market to be filled. This process of filling your order is known as "trade execution.[1]"

You should understand the types of orders before you place your trade. I will summarize them below, but if you would like to research them further I recommend reading the brief page on "Types of Order" available at investor.gov[2].

- A *market order* is an order to buy or sell a stock immediately. This type of order guarantees that the order will be executed, but does not guarantee the execution price. A market order generally will execute at or near the

current bid or ask price, but investors need to remember that the most recent price is not the price at which the market order will be executed. I feel this is a risky approach because it is like you are writing a blank check and market makers who place your trade have no limit to how much you will pay.
- A *limit order* is an order to buy or sell a security at a specific price or better. A buy limit order can only be executed at the limit price or lower, and a sell limit order can only be executed at the limit price or higher. Example: An investor wants to purchase shares of ABC stock for no more than $10. The investor could submit a limit order for this amount and this order will only execute if the price of ABC stock is $10 or lower[3]. I prefer limit orders because they give you control over what you pay for your shares and ensure you won't pay an infinite price.

The "pros" of market orders are that your order executes right away. The "cons" are that you have no control over the price at which your order is filled.

The "pros" of limit orders are that you have control over the buy or sell price at which you trade. The "cons" are that the quoted price may never reach the limit price you set and your trade will not execute.

A *market order* is like buying a car at a dealership if you walk in and agree to pay the sticker price of $30,000. You'll get the car immediately, but you might pay a lot for it. A *limit order* would be like telling the dealer you will only buy the car for $25,000 or less. You may or may not get the deal at your price, but you have control over the purchase price.

Real-life example

Here I will show you screenshots of an ETF purchase I made on March 12, 2020. I placed a limit order to buy 10 shares of the Vanguard

S&P 500 ETF at a share price of $230 or less.

I share these screenshots because I think it will be easier for you to understand if you can see real-life examples.

Steps to buying an ETF

This example shows the steps to buy shares of an S&P 500 ETF. This was an actual trade placed on March 12, 2020.

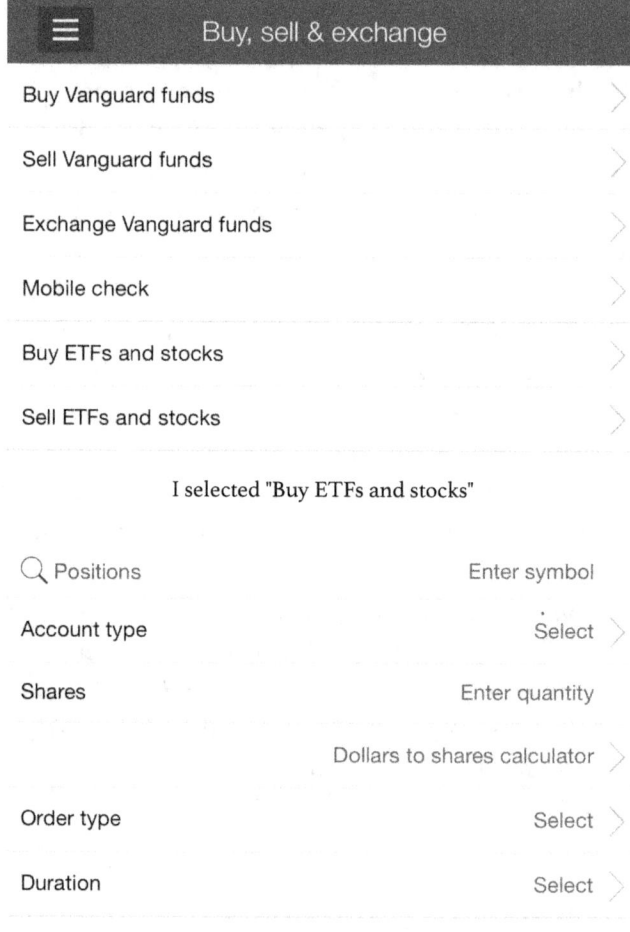

I selected "Buy ETFs and stocks"

I entered the ETF ticker symbol and how many shares I wanted to buy.

THE ETF INVESTOR

🔍 Positions	VOO
	Vanguard SP 500 ETF
Last trade	$229.54 -21.1917 (-8.45%)
OTC	03/12/2020 03:48 PM ET
Bid / Ask	$229.49 / $229.56
PSE PSE	
Size / Tick	3x5 / —
Volume	20,716,133

I entered the symbol VOO to buy shares of the Vanguard S&P 500 ETF.

🔍 Positions	VOO
	Vanguard SP 500 ETF
Last trade	$229.54 -21.1917 (-8.45%)
OTC	03/12/2020 03:48 PM ET
Bid / Ask	$229.49 / $229.56
PSE PSE	
Size / Tick	3x5 / —
Volume	20,716,133
Account type	Cash
Shares	10

I entered "10" because that's how many shares I wanted to buy.

Positions

VOO
Vanguard SP 500 ETF

Last trade	$229.54 -21.1917 (-8.45%)
OTC	03/12/2020 03:48 PM ET
Bid / Ask	$229.49 / $229.56
PSE PSE	
Size / Tick	3x5 / —
Volume	20,716,133
Account type	Cash
Shares	10
	Dollars to shares calculator >
Order type	Limit >

For "Order type" I selected "Limit" because that is the order type I prefer.

Positions

VOO
Vanguard SP 500 ETF

Last trade	$229.54 -21.1917 (-8.45%)
OTC	03/12/2020 03:48 PM ET
Bid / Ask	$229.49 / $229.56
PSE PSE	
Size / Tick	3x5 / —
Volume	20,716,133
Account type	Cash
Shares	10
	Dollars to shares calculator >
Order type	Limit >
Limit price	$230.00

Here is where I entered the limit price. This is the highest price I wanted to pay for shares. I entered $230.

THE ETF INVESTOR

Day >

60-day (GTC) >

Select trade duration — whether I wanted a "Day" order or valid for 60-day GTC which stands for "Good 'til canceled" which can execute any time within the next 60 days until canceled.

🔍 Positions	VOO
	Vanguard SP 500 ETF
Last trade	$229.54 -21.1917 (-8.45%)
OTC	03/12/2020 03:48 PM ET
Bid / Ask	$229.49 / $229.56
PSE PSE	
Size / Tick	3x5 / —
Volume	20,716,133
Account type	Cash
Shares	10
	Dollars to shares calculator >
Order type	Limit >
Limit price	$230.00
Duration	Day >

Quotes are shown in real time during regular trading hours. Market data provided by Thomson Reuters. Data are provided for information purposes only and are not intended for trading purposes. Thomson Reuters shall not be liable for any errors or any delay in the content, or for any action taken in reliance thereon. The RIC Thomson Reuters Instrument Code set has been developed and maintained by Thomson Reuters and is the intellectual property of Thomson Reuters. For additional quote information, go to the security profile page.

CANCEL   **CONTINUE**

This screen summarizes trade details. Check to ensure all details are accurate before proceeding.

Review and submit

ORDER SUMMARY

Shares	10
Order type	Limit
Limit price	$230.00
Duration	Day
Account type	Cash

ESTIMATED TRANSACTION DETAILS

Estimated principal	$2,300.00
Estimated commission	$0.00
Estimated net amount	$2,300.00

The commission and principal amounts are estimates. Market fluctuation, commission changes, availability of last price, or other changes may impact the final commission or principal amount. You'll receive final confirmation with transaction details for all executed trades.

Industry regulations require securities to be delivered on the settlement date. Vanguard reserves the right to reject your order at any time, for any reason, and without prior notice. If you continue this transaction, please monitor your order status to determine the final disposition of your order. You're liable for covering all transactions placed in this account. If you choose to exchange Vanguard funds into your money market settlement fund to cover this trade, you must complete the transaction no later than the business day before the settlement date. For market orders, you should consider price volatility when determining whether you'll have sufficient assets to pay for your purchase.

By clicking Submit, you consent to electronic access to the prospectus of the security you're purchasing. You may view and print the prospectus after submitting your order. If you would like an additional paper copy, please call Vanguard at 800-992-8327.

CANCEL   SUBMIT

Review and submit the order.

Transaction type	Buy
Symbol	VOO Vanguard S&P 500 ETF
Shares	10
Order type	Limit
Limit price	$230.00
Duration	Day
Account type	Cash

ESTIMATED TRANSACTION DETAILS

Estimated principal	$2,300.00
Estimated commission	$0.00
Estimated net amount	$2,300.00

After you submit the order you will receive a summary that acknowledges order receipt. At the top of the screen, it lists the name on the account, the order number, date, and time the order was placed. If the order executes at your limit price you will receive a trade confirmation.

Dow	Nasdaq	S&P500	
21322.41	7262.06	2497.71	
-2230.81 (-9.47%)	-689.99 (-8.68%)	-243.67 (-8.89%)	
VOO Vanguard S&P 500 ETF Bid: 228.59 x 1	228.57 12:57 PM Ask: 228.78 x 4	-22.16 -8.84%	
MSFT Microsoft Corporation Bid: 140.44 x 46	140.44 12:57 PM Ask: 140.34 x 4	-13.19 -8.59%	
AAPL Apple Inc Bid: 250.47 x 35	250.50 12:57 PM Ask: 250.52 x 2	-24.93 -9.05%	
AMZN Amazon.com, Inc Bid: 1684.36 x 1	1685.11 12:57 PM Ask: 1685.61 x 1	-135.75 -7.46%	
GOOG Alphabet Inc Bid: 1123.88 x 1	1124.04 12:57 PM Ask: 1124.64 x 1	-91.37 -7.52%	

I made this screenshot of my iPhone's stock tracking app (Stocks Tracker) right after I placed my trade. I placed a limit order at $230 and the actual share price was $228.57, which was below the price of my buy limit order and the trade executed.

If you have any questions about placing trades I recommend you call your brokerage firm's customer service phone number to get answers before trading.

As with anything new, learning about ETFs might seem a bit challenging at first, but after a while, it will become easy.

So, now that you have seen the steps involved in buying an ETF, the question remains: how often should you invest?

6
INVESTING AT INTERVALS

Invest a set amount over time

I think investing makes sense when you have a process. If you can schedule a date or time when you'll invest and stick to it you will ensure that you continue to invest over time.

Looking back on my investing history, I was a much better investor when I was just starting. As I mentioned earlier, I had a system where I invested $100 every month regardless of whether the market was up or down. This habit was easy enough that after a few months I increased my monthly investments to $200.

Monthly is easy

I think it would make sense to transfer $200 (or any amount you choose) from your bank account to your brokerage account every month. You can set up an automatic transfer from your bank to broker if you want to make sure it gets done. I like to make the transfer myself out of habit, but I'm thinking to automate this process so I don't have to remember to make the transfer every month to invest.

One thing I have learned from years of experience — and I'd like to share with you — is that *what you automate gets done.* If you have to remember to do something every month there might be times when work gets busy, or you're on vacation, and you just don't remember that monthly investment.

For years I paid my checks by check, and then by logging onto websites and making the payment manually. Life gets so much easier, and bills get paid on time when you set up automatic payments. Consider this reality to get money to your brokerage so you can invest at intervals. As long as the funds are there, it only takes a minute to buy an ETF.

The reason I like monthly investments is that saving $2,400 in a year is hard for many people to do in one "chunk." I know this was the case when I was getting started, and also I didn't like the risk of investing so much at high prices, so spreading out your purchases removes the chance of going "all in" on one day. Investing smaller amounts monthly may be easier when you're getting started.

Also, I'd like to put in a plug in for index funds (not ETFs) for readers who truly want to automate the process. You can actually set up monthly index fund purchases through a fund company or broker because they are *priced once* at the end of the day. This makes automatic purchases possible, whereas they are impossible with ETFs because their *prices fluctuate during the day* and the broker could not chose a purchase price for you.

Investing at regular intervals, through thick and thin (and especially through thin) worked out really well for me. I started this process with mutual funds and invested this way for nine years in a row, and the results from that system of monthly investments was outstanding.

I began investing every month for the five years leading up to the dot-com bust, and I continued for many years after. When tech stocks (and many others) crashed big time in 2000 and kept going down during 2001, 2002, and 2003, I kept investing. I bought every month when stocks were cheap and this mechanical monthly investment schedule (which took emotion out of the picture) provided good returns because I kept buying into the market when others were pessimistic and prices were cheap.

The investor and human behavior

Human error can derail even the best plans. Psychologist Daniel Kahneman won the Nobel Prize in economic sciences for applying psychological insights to economic theory, particularly in the areas of judgment and decision-making under uncertainty.

Kahneman's central message is that when humans are left to their own devices they are apt to engage in several human errors based on biases. To make better decisions, he said we ought to be aware of these biases and seek workarounds.[1] This is a powerful and important discovery.

Here's one story that shows how someone who realized his tendency to forget things figured out a workaround. One afternoon Dr. Drew Pinsky went to a radio station because he was going to be a guest on a radio show. Since he arrived a few minutes early he walked briskly into the kitchen and put a vial of insulin next to his car keys in the refrigerator.

Once the radio show began, the talk show host, Adam Carolla, told Pinsky he'd noticed the keys next to the insulin in the fridge, and because he knew Pinsky well, he knew instantly that the keys next to the insulin were to prevent him from driving off after the show and forgetting the insulin in the fridge.

Pinsky confirmed that was exactly the case: he needed to deliver the insulin to a patient after the show, but needed it to remain cold in the meantime. He knew he'd probably jump in his car after the show and leave the insulin behind.

So, to make sure that didn't happen, Pinsky put his car keys next to the insulin so it would be impossible to drive off without first stopping off at the fridge.

I like this example of finding a workaround to conquer forgetfulness. I remember this story even though I heard the radio show years ago because it shows how a smart person who is aware of his tendency toward human error can find a workaround.

I use this key trick when I don't want to forget something. I have a large carabiner[2] on my keychain, and I attach it to anything I don't want to forget when I leave the house. It's been a real game-changer.

We all have tendencies to make mistakes or forget things, and I find that ETFs simplify investing because they make it easy to buy shares with your phone or broker's website. This ease of use simplifies periodic investing.

Is it possible to become an intelligent investor with just one ETF?

7

SIMPLICITY WITH ONE ETF

You can keep things simple by investing in just one ETF and then buying more shares at regular intervals.

The beauty of ETFs is their ability to let you buy a diverse collection of assets in just one trade.

Let's start by looking at a few options.

S&P 500 ETF

This is a good place to start when considering an ETF. In one simple fund you own part of the 500 largest companies in the US, and it's dirt cheap. You get an extremely diversified investment and it's practically free to buy because most ETFs trade commission-free.

JEFF LUKE

A piñata is a perfect symbol for an S&P 500 ETF because it's one large package made up of many small parts. Artwork by Edwin Yaguar Chávez

Here is an example of the holdings of a typical S&P 500 ETF. This happens to be Vanguard's offering, but as you will soon see, the long-term returns among similar funds are identical.

Vanguard S&P 500 ETF (VOO)

10 Largest Holdings[1]
  Expense ratio: .03%
  Holding | %

  1. Microsoft Corp. 5.60%
  2. Apple Inc. 4.90%
  3. Amazon.com Inc. 3.80%
  4. Alphabet Inc. 3.20%
  5. Facebook Inc. 1.90%

6. Berkshire Hathaway Inc. 1.70%
7. Johnson & Johnson 1.60%
8. Visa Inc. 1.30%
9. Procter & Gamble Co. 1.30%
10. JPMorgan Chase & Co. 1.20%

There are other ETFs similar to Vanguard's (VOO) such as State Street's SPDR® S&P 500® ETF (SPY) and Blackrock's iShares S&P 500 (IVV). The graph and table below show their identical returns over the past 10 years.

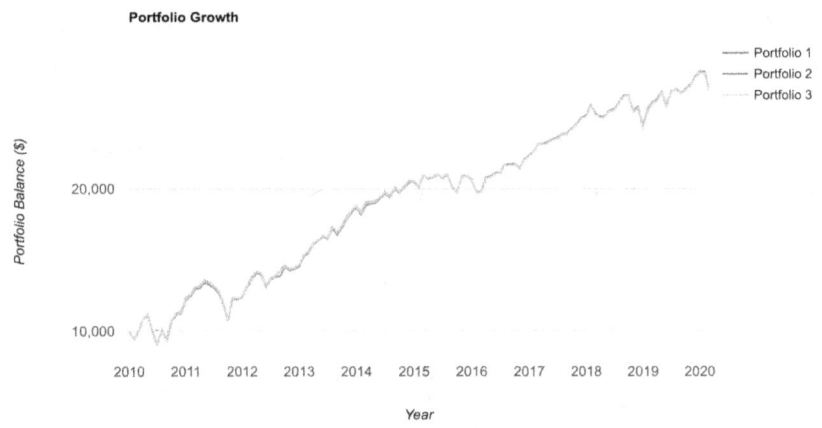

Chart of VOO, SPY, and IVV. Source: Portfolio Visualizer

Though it may appear that you're only looking at one line above, I assure you that those are three overlapping lines representing ETFs that own the same 500 stocks. This underscores the similar returns of ETFs that track the same index with low costs.

Throughout this book when comparing funds using a graph like the one above I will also include a table of ETF returns so you can easily see the relevant data.

This table lists the ETF ticker (a unique identifying symbol), the starting amount of a hypothetical investment, the ending amount of that investment after 10 years, and the compound annual growth rate (CAGR)[2].

Symbol | Initial Balance | Final Balance | CAGR

- Portfolio 1 - VOO $10,000 $28,262 10.67%
- Portfolio 2 - SPY $10,000 $28,429 10.73%
- Portfolio 3 - IVV $10,000 $28,518 10.76%

There is an annual expense to own ETF shares, and these are expressed as a percentage of your investment. For example, the fund above charges a .03% expense ratio which means that if you have $1,000 invested the expense is $.30 a year. For a $10,000 investment, the expense is $3.00 a year.

Think about that: Index-based ETFs let you buy slices of the 500 largest US companies for less than the price of a double tall mocha with whip.

A piñata holds a variety of candies, just as an index fund holds a variety of stocks. Artwork by Edwin Yaguar Chávez.

THE ETF INVESTOR

Total stock market ETFs

These ETFs include small-cap and mid-cap stocks as well as large caps[3]. Vanguard Total Stock Market ETF (VTI) owns 3,535 stocks, Schwab U.S. Broad Market ETF (SCHB) owns 2,445 stocks, and iShares Total Stock Market (ITOT) owns 3,632 stocks.

Three options to consider:

- Vanguard Total Stock Market ETF (VTI)
- The SPDR S&P 1500 (SCHB)
- iShares Total Stock Market (ITOT)

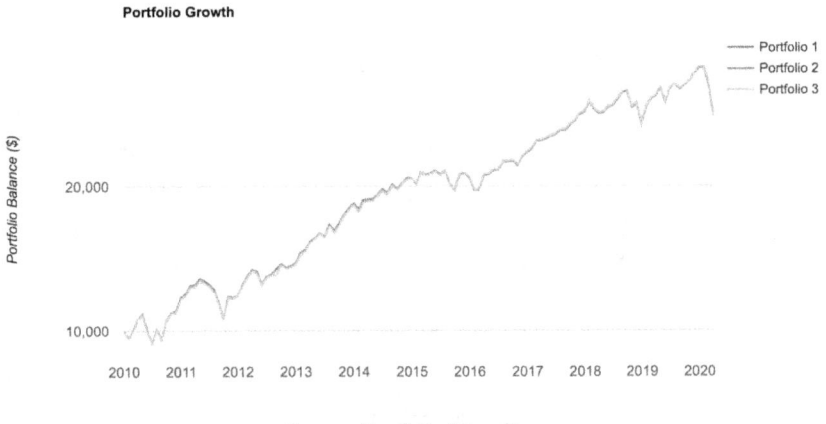

Source: Portfolio Visualizer

Though this chart appears to show a single line, you are looking at three overlapping lines. The total returns of all three ETFs are identical.

Portfolio | Initial Balance | Final Balance | CAGR

- Portfolio 1 (VTI) $10,000 $27,903 10.53%
- Portfolio 2 (SCHB) $10,000 $27,819 10.50%

35

- Portfolio 3 (ITOT) $10,000 $27,974 10.56%

As you can see, these ETFs have generated identical returns over the past decade.

Own the Whole World

There are three large global stock ETFs that provide exposure to companies all over the world. QWLD, URTH, and VT have thousands of holdings and provide wide diversification. If you want to buy only one ETF, any of these broadly diversified funds will fit the bill.[4]

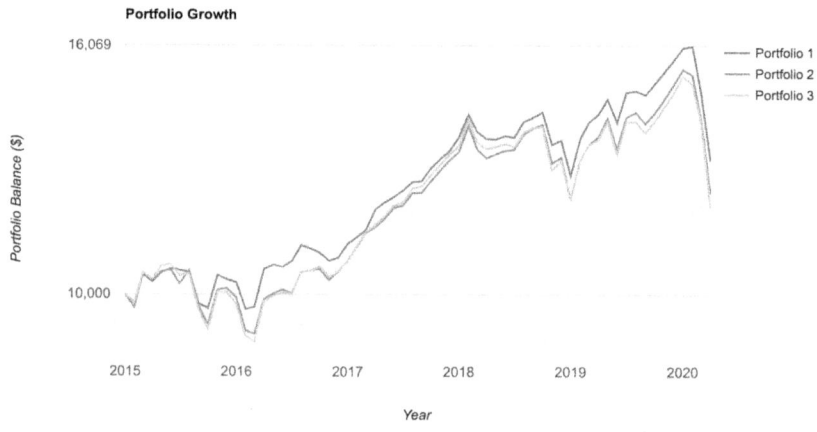

Source: Portfolio Visualizer

Portfolio | Initial Balance | Final Balance | CAGR

- Portfolio 1 - QWLD $10,000 $12,901 4.97%
- Portfolio 2 - URTH $10,000 $12,119 3.73%
- Portfolio 3 - VT $10,000 $11,812 3.22%

I hope this section has helped you realize that one ETF can be perfectly sufficient.

However, if you're like me and like to know some of the other items on the menu before you order, then you've come to the right place.

In the next chapter, we'll take a look at ETFs that invest in stock market niches.

How many ETFs does an investor need?

More is not necessarily better with ETFs. You might think that you'll get better results by owning many different ETFs, each one investing in a different sector, style, or geographic location.

I don't think there is any guarantee you will get better results by owning many ETFs. It can make sense — if you like the process — to choose a few different ETFs to gain exposure to different parts of the stock market. If you choose this path, I think it makes sense to make sure new ETFs don't overlap too much with what you already own. This way each new investment diversifies your portfolio.

However, if you're just starting out, it is not necessary to invest in several ETFs. It can feel overwhelming at times, and you just don't need that kind of stress in your life. Each investor is different, and while some people might fear picking several ETFs, others might like the challenge of picking different ETFs for emerging markets, small companies, energy stocks, tech stocks, cryptocurrencies, fintech, gold, real estate, dividend-paying stocks, international stocks, internet stocks, etc.

Adding more ETFs won't guarantee better long-term results. There is no way to know which market sector, asset class, or investment style will perform best in the future.

Several years ago I started investing in international mutual funds that own stocks in companies based in Brazil, China, Great Britain, France, India, Japan, Korea, Russia, Saudi Arabia, Switzerland, Taiwan, Thailand, and many other countries. I invested in these funds because I thought the US, being a mature nation, would grow more slowly fast growing economies in other parts of the world.

One of the mutual funds has an ETF equivalent, the Vanguard

Emerging Markets fund (VWO). Now, in theory, I like the idea of owning stock in companies like fast-growing Alibaba and Tencent.

Though I've mentioned many nations above, the largest companies, which are the top holdings in VWO, are based in China and Taiwan. Seven of the top 10 companies are in those two countries...*so much for diversification!*)

That emerging markets fund has been a drag on performance for more than 10 years I've owned it. $10,000 would have *tripled the return* to $36,488 in a S&P 500 index ETF and only grew to $13,551 in VWO.

So, as you can see, sometimes diversification into new ETFs does not help you at all. It can greatly slow down the growth of your investment.

However, I am guilty of looking in the rear-view mirror! During the past decade it is very possible that international companies, (including those in China and Taiwan in that VWO ETF) have been growing and becoming profitable, and all the while their stocks have been undervalued. Meanwhile, the stock market in the United States has become insanely expensive.

It is entirely possible that things could turn around in the next few years and international stocks will come into favor. I am not selling my international funds, because the day I do *I just know* international stocks will roar back!

It's really a personal choice, and only you know whether you like the simplicity provided by just one, or a few ETFs, or whether you like to adventure out and buy several. I think it makes sense to start with one, and once you get comfortable with the process you can always add more.

It's hard to beat the S&P

If you want proof of how hard it is to beat the market, look no further than the fact that most professional investors fail to beat the returns of the S&P 500 index[5].

Even Warren Warren Buffett admitted on CNBC that he's had a "tough time" trying to beat the S&P 500, and he said that his two

THE ETF INVESTOR

investing lieutenants, Ted Weschler and Todd Combs, have each underperformed the S&P 500 during the past few years by a "tiny bit." Even so, he added that their stock picks have done better than his[6].

One approach to ETF investing could be to start with one diversified ETF like those described above as your "core" holding and then invest in other ETFs if you want to focus on sectors or assets to supplement your core ETF.

Are you curious about other ETFs to investigate further? I list 23 that catch my attention in upcoming chapters.

8

ETFS HELP YOU KEEP CALM

ETFs let you relax because with them you don't need to pick the perfect stocks. Instead, you can invest in a collection of stocks with just one investment. This greatly *simplifies* a process that can be mentally difficult for many people to begin that they'd rather do anything to avoid it.

I know this from personal experience. If you have money set aside that you know you need to invest for your future self, you don't want to screw up and pick the wrong stock. "Analysis paralysis" sets in and you might find yourself making lists of stocks, or following several watchlist portfolios on your phone or computer, thinking about the pros and cons for each stock. If you choose the wrong stock you could lose money big time, or if you never decide on a stock then your money just sits there in a cash account earning nothing.

Then, while you're waiting, you see another exciting stock, and the process begins again. You start thinking about putting the money into some other stock and you spend hours researching it late into the night. Yet you never actually accomplish the serious work of putting a big chunk of money into an investment for future you.

ETFs worked for me in 2020

As I mentioned earlier in this book, I had no experience with ETF investing when I started writing this book. I had invested for years in index funds, which are closely related to ETFs, but trade differently. I share this with you because if you're just starting, I want you to know that you can get up and running without a lot of training and you'll do just fine.

The simplicity of ETFs — which trade just as easily as stocks — is that when the pandemic hit, I was able to make a few courageous buys while the world was collapsing around me like Tyler Durden[1].

There's a quote from Fight Club that reflects this attitude: "Only after disaster can we be resurrected. It's only after you've lost everything that you're free to do anything. Nothing is static, everything is evolving, everything is falling apart."

Invest when everything falls apart

Yes, you can invest during the uncertainty of life, disaster, and evolution. It is rare that you will have many chances to invest when the world seems to be falling apart. You may have a few such opportunities to be decisive at these times, and picking individual stocks can be difficult at these times.

When the virus-induced mayhem caused markets to fall like dominoes across the world, stocks were red for days and weeks at a time. While others were panic selling, I *knew that I should not fear get in the way*. It was ingrained in my thinking that the best times to invest is when others are fearful, and ETFs made this a breeze.

So, that's what I want readers to know as we proceed. ETFs don't require you to know a lot about individual stocks. As I mentioned earlier, I had no experience investing with ETFs when I started writing this book, yet I was able to invest successfully even at a time of maximum chaos and market volatility. ETFs made investing very easy.

1. ETFs provide stock ownership in one easy investment.

2. With EFTs you don't have to time the market.
3. You can invest in ETFs as part of a long-term process.

Bear markets teach you something

I was listening to the Rational Reminder podcast recently, and the guest, Kenneth French, said that bear markets teach you something about yourself.[2]

Speaking of investing amidst the volatility surrounding the pandemic he said, "The reason one might want to adjust his or her portfolio at this point is *because they've learned something about themselves*," he said. French said that during the pandemic, people learned that their tolerance for risk *was lower than they thought*. "If that's really the case, *then fine!*" French suggested that if people aren't comfortable with a high level of volatility and the experience is more painful than anticipated — it can make sense to adjust your portfolio.

Most people handle markets going up just fine, but I've observed that some people get stressed out when markets crash. We all have different emotional experiences when we perceive gains and losses. Investing teaches us lessons by direct experience what we can't learn by pondering hypothetical situations. Other people seem to have the DNA to withstand volatility and not think twice; if this includes you, consider yourself fortunate. Your steady temperament will allow you to hold stocks when people around you are losing their minds.

As you read through this book, keep in mind that some ETFs discussed will perform similarly to the stock market indexes if they track one, or their performance might fluctuate wildly from the overall market.

Only you can know if you prefer to just buy and hold a broad market index ETF for a long time, or if you prefer to try to take on extra risk in an attempt to beat the market.

You can think of this as two types of boats, a small racing sailboat, and a huge cargo ship. The racing boat is lightweight and made to go fast, and it cuts through the water quickly and is made for speed. It could easily capsize or be damaged by big waves or winds that batter and damage its sails or lightweight mast or boom; it is sensitive to its surroundings.

The large cargo ship is made to transport cars, trucks, and huge containers of goods through all kinds of storms and inclement weather. It's not going to set any speed records or win races, but it will likely keep stable despite turbulence despite wind and water turbulence.

As you browse ETFs in this book keep this in mind - some investments may focus on fast growth and be extremely sensitive to the stock market's gyrations, while others may be diversified and spread across many countries, companies, or industries and less sensitive to any one factor.

9

FACTOR INVESTING

Factor investing has become popular in recent years. Online message boards and financial advising podcasts shine a spotlight on research that suggests any ways that investors can get stock returns over what the overall market provides.

The world of academic investing is dominated by two names, Eugene Fama and Kenneth French. Intelligent and methodical as they are in their approaches, their approaches are not adopted by all. Instead, their approach has been confined to economists, financial advisers, and authors who deliberate on the best way to obtain "alpha."[1]

Many good investors ignore their theories entirely and dismiss them as useless, while others quote them at every turn. "Factor investing" has become popularized by a paper that Fama and French authored[2], and it has become more popular in many conversations that revolve around creating investment portfolios that generate alpha. Those investors chasing alpha dive deep into the waters of investing in search of the rare catch, a perfect investment into an asset class that provides excess returns without added risk. This has resulted in a search for an ETF (or a few) that provides exposure to that holy grail at a low cost.

I didn't know about Fama and French until recently; I never took college courses about investing, nor have I used academic principles to guide my investing. While learning about their research has not changed my investing in any significant way, I will say that I have taken an even harder look at small-cap ETFs now that I'm aware of their strong long-term performance, something reinforced by Fama and French's research.

However, even though I don't consider myself a factor investing fanatic, *I do think readers can benefit from understanding* that careful academic research does support the notion that *small-cap stocks*, particularly small-cap *value* stocks, might "tilt" long-term returns in their favor. Small-cap stocks may provide investors with a welcome addition if they want to try to squeeze a little excess return out of their portfolios, especially if they already own large-cap stocks or funds.

There is no guarantee that the next 20 years will provide the same type of returns as the past (and there's a good chance they won't), but if past is prologue, small-cap ETFs *might* boost a portfolio's returns above those of the market averages.[3]

As you read about the many ETFs in this book it might help you to frame it this way: You can already own broad exposure to the stock market's returns using just one ETF as we saw in an earlier chapter.

With very little effort you can get a perfectly decent result by harnessing the stock market's return in a low-cost way. As you invest in other ETFs, your portfolio can become more or less sensitive to the overall stock market depending on how your exposure; let's look at a couple of examples.

Example of extreme portfolio tilt

To give you an extreme example that is all over the financial news lately, let's look at people who invest in Bitcoin. Investors who recently put a chunk of their money into Bitcoin have seen it grow in price rapidly. So, we can see the incredibly fast growth of this particular asset has affected the overall portfolio value...in the upward direction[4].

But there is a tradeoff: Bitcoin could crash and suddenly the overall portfolio value would drop because of the exposure to Bitcoin. I use this example from a neutral position — it's neither praising nor hating on Bitcoin — it's just pointing out that investors who "tilt" their portfolio toward it will benefit strongly if it continues to grow in price, and it will detract if the price declines.

The same can be said of a stock like Tesla, which has increased 1,383.07% in the past five years.[5] There are a lot of people who got rich buying Tesla stock a few years ago. If an investor tilted their portfolios toward Tesla they observed a rapid gain in overall value. However, their portfolios are sensitive to changes in Tesla's stock price. They could get even richer, or they could suddenly find themselves with a much lower net worth.

So, the take-home message here is that a tilt toward, or *exposure* to Bitcoin or Tesla can have a massive impact on a portfolio's returns.

These extreme examples show you how "factor" investing works. By holding many different assets, ETFs provide more diversification than one would get from a single asset like Bitcoin or stock like Tesla. However, if you buy an ETF that focuses on one segment of the market or an asset class like small-cap value, you will have more exposure, and thus more sensitivity, to that part of the market.

The question to ask yourself at every turn is, "How will putting money into a specific part of the market affect my portfolio's returns over time?"

Factor investing in a nutshell

You can go very far down the rabbit hole of academic investing, so far that your brain will get confused when considering "asset pricing models" and *you won't know what to do*. I heard an excellent interview with professor Kenneth French[6] in which he discussed his financial advisor, and said the relationship is valuable to him.

I enjoyed this podcast, and I think it's worth noting that even the king of academic investing research consults with a financial advisor. This reveals two noteworthy details.

1. Even smart and experienced investors feel they benefit from an objective opinion about their finances.
2. The "Factor Investing" that French teaches at Dartmouth College is not so simple that he can implement his investment decisions by himself.

There is a lot of *thinking* involved in the academic investing process, and *this doesn't necessarily make investing easier*. I think over-analysis of these factors can work against an investor because you can either get *confused* and not know where to start, or cause them to invest in many different vehicles whose effects cancel each other out.

Still, I think it's worth knowing the basic message of the academics, which is that you can "tilt" your investment portfolio to take advantage of investment *factors* such as small companies vs. large companies, or growth vs. value.

For example, if you invest in an ETF that buys large companies you may have different returns than if you invest in one that invests in small companies.

Similarly, if you invest in ETFs filled with "growth" stocks your investments may perform differently than if you invest in ETFs that invest in "value" stocks. In a nutshell, growth stocks generally are faster growing and more expensive because their prices take into account expectations for faster growth and more money in the future. Value stocks are often cheaper because investors don't expect them to make as much money, and as a result, their stock prices are cheaper.

What is the optimal asset class for investors? Large or small company, growth or value? You'll get a different answer depending on who you ask. The investing climate also greatly influences attitudes toward asset classes. The state of the economy, market momentum, and emotions of the crowds all drive market prices and fluctuate from year to year for reasons that are often unclear. In other words, nobody knows for sure which asset classes (or ETFs) will perform best in the future.

So, I think you will benefit from knowing about these different investing factors because they come to play whenever you make an ETF investment in a sector or specific kind of stock in hopes of beating the market's return.

Also, if you're ever talking with friends about investing you can say you cite your reason for picking an ETF by casually mentioning, "I invested in this small caps EFT because in their 2014 research paper, "A Five-Factor Asset Pricing Model,"[7] Fama and French said their new model shows that the highest expected returns are attained by companies that are small, profitable and value companies with no major growth prospects. A nice bit of name-dropping, and your friends will instantly know you're an expert who's on top of the latest academic research.

Now that you're familiar with the different factors and methods by which you can "tilt" your returns, let's take a look at ETFs that provide stock exposure to help you reach your investing goals.

10

THE 25 ETFS

I will share with you the ETFs that caught my eye while writing this book. I bought shares in two of these ETFs based on my research, and I'm thinking to add another soon.

I think you might discover some new ideas for future investments, and in the pages to come you'll get an idea of why some of these ETFs might help you to invest.

In creating this list I aimed to include a variety of different ETFs because each person reading this might have a different style as an investor, or be comfortable with varying degrees of volatility from day-to-day.

Investors come in all colors and stripes. While I own a couple of these (and I will disclose which ones and tell you why I like them), but you should keep in mind that I have no crystal ball to predict future performance, and my owning something should have no bearing on your decisions[1].

To give you an idea of why I share many funds that I don't invest in myself: if I showed you *only ETFs I find of interest* there's a chance I'd omit useful funds due to my own biases. I might look at some ETF and say, "I'd never buy that, therefore it's a dumb and stupid ETF that should not exist," yet you might take a look and think it would be a great addition to your portfolio because of your interests, style, or comfort level with a sector or company size.

So, to counter my own biases, I'm sharing with you a selection of ETFs that I feel are remarkable — either because I think they focus on an interesting segment, or their portfolio provides exposure to a part of the market that you can't get easily with a market-based index fund.

Whether you're an investor who simply wants exposure to the stock market for long-term investing, or you hope to squeeze out excess return from the market from your strategic selections, I hope you find some new investing ideas in these pages that you might not have discovered on your own.

11

SMALL-CAP ETFS

When I first wrote about ETFs in "The ETF Investor" in early 2020, small-cap stocks had anemic returns compared to large-cap growth powerhouse stocks like Alphabet, Amazon, Apple, Facebook, Microsoft, NVIDIA, and Tesla.

The mega-growth stocks had dominated the US economy as the darlings of the stock market for years. With many working from home during the pandemic, these tech companies increased their dominance. Even casual observers knew that large tech companies drive the stock market.

Yet, as I sit down one year later to write about ETFs I see massive change: suddenly, *small-cap ETFs*, particularly small-cap *value* ETFs, have sprung back mightily with returns of *30% to more than 40% in only four months*.

Let me take a moment to share my interest in small-cap ETFs. I did not own any small-cap funds at the beginning of 2020, and when the pandemic hit I invested first in VOO (the S&P 500 index) during the March crash.

As the market continued to decline, I decided to invest in small-caps because they were getting hammered and becoming cheap. I would guess this happened because people were afraid these small companies would not do well during the pandemic.

Now, you should know that total market index funds (like those described in an earlier chapter) *include* small-cap stocks, they exist as a *much smaller weighting* compared to large-caps. By investing directly into a small-cap ETF I could ensure I was getting pure small-cap exposure and I could buy as much as I want — without buying tons of large-cap stocks along with them.

Also, I should just make sure to explain what I mean by "small-cap" ETFs—the terms "large-cap," "mid-cap," and "small-cap" for investors who are just getting started. These are terms that describe company size. The "cap" part stands for capitalization, calculated by multiplying total shares outstanding by stock price[1].

I want this book you're reading to provide a complete picture of ETFs available, and this *must include ETFs that invest in a variety of asset classes*. In this chapter, we'll focus on small-cap companies, which means companies with market caps between $300 million and $2 billion[2].

To give you a point of reference, Apple's market cap is just over $2 trillion, Disney's market cap is $333 billion, Nike's is $207 billion, Starbucks' is $134 billion, and Tesla's is $641 billion. As you can see, a company smaller than $2 billion is *tiny* compared to the big dogs, which means these stocks are often more volatile, and over long periods they can potentially grow faster than larger, more established companies.[3]

Keep in mind that the small-cap funds in this chapter include both "growth" and "value" stocks. As a quick refresher, *growth stocks* usually have higher prices because they are expected to grow profits rapidly in the future. We could say these companies have higher *expected returns*.

Value stocks, on the other hand, have lower prices because they are not expected to exhibit rapid growth, or because they are in less glamorous industries in which demand for their products or services is low. Ideally, an investor should aim to pay *less* and get more in return. For this reason, *low valuation* (or cheap) stocks make sense to value investors because they don't like to pay high prices for the value they receive in exchange for the dollars they invest. Growth investors, on the other hand, are often not too concerned if the price is high, because they believe the high stock price reflects optimism about a company's *future growth*.

I know this may seem like a lot to digest if you're a new investor, but eventually it will make sense. Think of this explanation as early exposure, like a vaccine that will help you prepare to understand "growth" and "value" the next time you see these words describing a fund. If you already know about valuation, then this serves as your refresher.

Growth and value are *simply ways of grouping companies* based on valuation, but *neither category is better* than the other. Growth might be in fashion for years at a time, then suddenly the stock market "rotates" and value comes into style. It's impossible to predict the timing of these changes.

Also, keep in mind that company size often changes: small-cap companies are often start-ups that are growing rapidly may soon be mid caps or even large caps one day. Others have been small for years and will likely remain small for many more. These companies often produce just one product or service, and they tend to lack the economic stability of larger companies to withstand shocks to the economy or recessions.

Small caps are often considered "riskier" investments, but I don't worry about investing in small-cap ETFs because I believe the risk of one company in the ETF failing is not a problem because there are so many of them which dilute the impact of any single company. This is excellent for us as investors, and you can think of it as getting *exposure to an asset class* with greatly *diminished exposure to any one stock*.

Let's look at a few small cap ETFs below, and I'll provide comments on distinguishing characteristics, some pros and cons, and useful data on returns.[4]

By the way, one useful source of ETF information is "ETF Database" at the website ETFdb.com. You will find information about this website and others in the "Useful Resources" section at the end of this book. ETF Database provides a ton of useful data on a wide variety of ETFs. They have tools like an ETF screener and a head-to-head comparison tool. If you decide to use this website, look for the small magnifying glass in the top right corner of each page to search for individual ETFs. I find this website to be useful when I want to check an ETFs top holdings and expenses. I also like the "head to head" comparison tool.

You can also research ETFs on Yahoo Finance and Morningstar. You may want to check with your local library to see if your library subscribes to Morningstar's premium database service. My local library provides this to members free and it's worth checking out.

Another way to search is simply to type the ticker symbol into Google or any search engine and the letters ETF. For example, for the ETF listed below, typing "VB ETF" will provide you with plenty of useful information.

Vanguard Small-Cap ETF (VB)

Top 15 Holdings
Expense ratio: .05%
Symbol / Holding / % Assets

1. LDOS Leidos Holdings Inc 0.49%
2. STE Steris plc 0.47%
3. DOCU DocuSign Inc 0.46%
4. ATO Atmos Energy Corp 0.44%
5. WST West Pharmaceutical Services Inc 0.44%
6. TDY Teledyne Technologies Inc 0.43%
7. TYL Tyler Technologies Inc 0.43%
8. IEX IDEX Corp 0.42%
9. ZBRA Zebra Technologies Corp 0.39%
10. TDOC Teladoc Health Inc 0.38%
11. PODD Insulet Corp 0.38%
12. BAH Booz Allen Hamilton Holding Corp 0.38%
13. ELS Equity LifeStyle Properties Inc 0.37%

14. TER Teradyne Inc 0.37%
15. VICI VICI Properties Inc 0.36%

Number of Holdings: 1330
% of Assets in Top 15: 6.40%

iShares Core S&P Small-Cap ETF (IJR)

IJR is a solid choice for a small-cap ETF because it screens new holdings for profitability and it weeds out some stocks that the fund committee believes will help the fund match the S&P SmallCap 600 Index[5].

Top 15 Holdings
Expense ratio: .07%
Symbol / Company / % Assets

1. LHCG LHC Group Inc 0.73%
2. EXPO Exponent Inc 0.70%
3. CCOI Cogent Communications Holdings Inc 0.67%
4. NEOG Neogen Corp 0.63%
5. BCPC Balchem Corp 0.60%
6. CBU Community Bank System Inc 0.60%
7. AJRD Aerojet Rocketdyne Holdings Inc 0.58%
8. MNTA Momenta Pharmaceuticals Inc 0.57%
9. QLYS Qualys Inc 0.57%
10. AWR American States Water Co 0.56%
11. EHTH eHealth Inc 0.56%
12. ADC Agree Realty Corp 0.55%
13. OMCL Omnicell Inc 0.54%
14. GBCI Glacier Bancorp Inc 0.54%
15. STRA Strategic Education Inc 0.53%

Number of Holdings: 602
% of Assets in Top 15: 8.90%

Schwab U.S. Small-Cap ETF (SCHA)

This is another solid ETF for small-cap stocks. It seeks to match the total return of the Dow Jones U.S. Small-Cap Total Stock Market. This ETF offers a broad, market-cap-weighted portfolio and a low expense ratio of .04%[6].

Top 15 Holdings[7]
Expense ratio: .04%
Symbol / Holding / % Assets

1. Cash Component Cash Component 1.07%
2. MRNA Moderna Inc 0.58%
3. TDOC Teladoc Health Inc 0.56%
4. IR Ingersoll Rand Inc 0.44%
5. ETSY ETSY Inc 0.42%
6. HZNP Horizon Therapeutics PLC 0.35%
7. CRL Charles River Laboratories International Inc 0.34%
8. ENTG Entegris Inc 0.33%
9. CIEN Ciena Corp 0.32%
10. ZNGA Zynga Inc 0.32%
11. CHGG Chegg Inc 0.32%
12. TREX Trex Company Inc 0.29%
13. GNRC Generac Holdings Inc 0.28%
14. IMMU Immunomedics Inc 0.28%
15. FIVN Five9 Inc 0.28%

Number of Holdings: 1711
% of Assets in Top 15: 6.16%

THE ETF INVESTOR

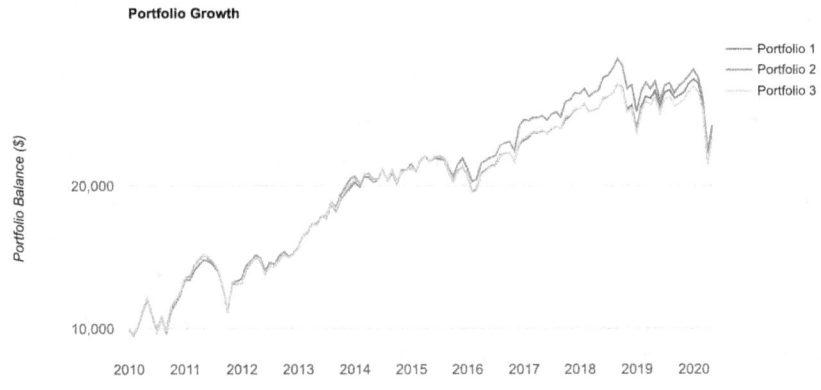

Three small-cap ETFs. Source: Portfolio Visualizer

This chart shows the performance of these three small-cap ETFs over 10-years, and they all delivered similar returns.

Portfolio | Initial Balance | Final Balance | CAGR

- Portfolio 1 - VB $10,000 $26,759 9.99%
- Portfolio 2 - IJR $10,000 $26,568 9.92%
- Portfolio 3 - SCHA $10,000 $25,352 9.42%

Many of the stocks held in these small-cap ETFs are not yet robust enough to withstand competition or shocks to the economy because they may only have one product or service that can make the company vulnerable during a pandemic, recession, or any other exogenous event.

Small-cap stocks tend to be riskier than their large-cap counterparts. However, these funds' broad reach helps them diminish company-specific risks and provides investors with exposure to the small-cap segment of the market.

As I mentioned earlier, all three ETFs listed above (and many similar ETFs) provide investors with exposure to companies that are not typically included in large-cap investment portfolios like the S&P 500.

During times of uncertainty, these small-cap ETFs might fall in price faster than larger, more established companies. However, when the economy is in recovery or growth mode, it's often small caps that lead the way.

There are risks and benefits to owning small company ETFs, but the only thing you can say for sure is they can diversify your portfolio and decrease overall risk. This is especially useful if you already own large-cap stocks or index funds and ETFs that invest heavily in large companies.

For example, I own some mutual funds and ETFs and they all invest in large companies. Some of them are S&P 500 funds and others are global, international, or large-cap value funds. But the bottom line is that almost all of my investments are in stocks of large companies.

There's nothing wrong with owning all of these large companies, but I have decided that I wanted to invest in smaller companies too. That's where VB, IJR, and SCHA can be useful — as a way of getting some diversification in portfolio dominated by large-cap stocks.

As of this writing on April 30, 2021 the year-to-date return for VB is 16.24%, IJR is 22.21% and SCHA 17.16%[8], so you can see that all three ETFs delivered similar YTD returns. Of course, no one can predict which of these three funds will outperform in the future. Looking at an ETF's performance over only four months is does not give us useful information, but it does show how short-term performance can be influenced by the size of companies in a portfolio.

It is useful to not that between January and April of 2021 *small cap-stocks* outperformed large-cap stocks, and *value* outperformed growth. The return for IJR is 5-6% greater than the other funds during this period. If you wonder why, this is most likely explained by the different benchmarks that each of these funds seeks to match. VB uses the CRSP US Small-Cap Index, IJR uses the S&P SmallCap 600 Index, and SCHW uses the Dow Jones U.S. Small-Cap Total Stock

Market Total Return Index. Each ETF tracks a different index, and this accounts for their YTD differences.

It's worth pointing out that as of April 30, 2021—just four months into the year—small-cap ETFs with the *tiniest* companies appreciated most in price. As small businesses shifted into high gear, investors plowed money into the smallest companies in the stock market.

This may explain why IJR outperformed the two other ETFs mentioned above by a significant margin: it tracks the **S&P SmallCap 600 index** as its benchmark, an index of companies with an *average size of $1.8 billion*.[9]

If you look at VB, you will see that it tracks the **CRSP US Small-Cap Index**[10] as its benchmark. This index invests in companies with an *average size of $3.7 billion*[11] Although VB is categorized as a small-cap ETF, the index it tracks has a market-cap *twice as large* as IJR's.

As a result, while VB has returned more than the S&P 500 as of April 30, 2021, it has underperformed IJR, which holds *smaller companies* on average.

However, if we look at a 3-year period, VB (58%) has outperformed IJR (49%) because larger companies performed better (especially the largest companies like Amazon, Apple, Alphabet, Microsoft, etc) compared to smaller companies. It follows that in this environment, small-cap ETFs holding larger stocks (VB) would perform better than those holding smaller stocks (IJR). Stock returns fluctuate wildly and may favor one ETF over short periods and another over longer periods.[12]

I *knew* I wanted to buy shares of a small-cap ETF during the Corona Crash, and when the stock market fell in March of 2020 and the prices of all stocks cratered, I decided to invest in a small-cap ETF for the first time. I chose VB because it's cheap and provides inexpensive exposure to the asset class, but *any* of the small-cap ETFs mentioned earlier in this chapter would have done the trick.

A rocket scientist on small cap stocks

William Bengen provided insights on how much investors can safely withdraw from their retirement accounts when they retire when he was a guest on the Rational Reminder Podcast.[13] Bengen received a B.S. from MIT in Aeronautics and Astronautics, so he is was literally a rocket scientist who practiced financial planning for over 25 years.[14]

You may wonder why a book about ETFs would suddenly discuss retirement planning, and no, I'm not trying to make readers fall asleep. Bengen made an observation about asset allocation decisions that investors made when they were young that gave them great benefits when they retired. Since many readers are likely years from retirement I think there is considerable value to sharing Bengen's observation. This one type of stock — which you can buy in an ETF — has historically added a noticeable return to investment accounts, retirement or otherwise.

Before diving into his revelation, I'd like to share Bengen's contribution to retirement planning so you'll know the kind of "stress-testing" he has done to determine how much money retirees can safely withdraw from their investment portfolios under different economic conditions. He used data from different periods, market cycles, and inflation scenarios to see how well investments held up under a variety of scenarios.[15]

Bengen's research-based approach to withdrawal rates opens up new doors that help investors make intelligent decisions that aren't based on "gut feelings." When he worked as a financial planner his specialty was advising people on prospective withdrawal rates. In other words, how much money could you safely withdraw from your investments over 30 or 40 years (or longer) and *not run out of money*.

Bengen said that using several asset classes can benefit investors and spoke to the benefits of a well-diversified portfolio. Speaking about small-cap stocks, Bengen said, "I chose them as kind of a proxy for a lot of other asset classes one, *because they had a higher rate of return than large-cap stocks* —by about 2%—so they're adding return,

THE ETF INVESTOR

and they didn't have a perfect correlation to large-cap stocks, so *they added some diversification value.*"

In that simple statement Bengen gives two strong reasons investors may want to consider the small-cap exposure they can get through an ETF.

Small-Cap vs Large-Cap Stocks 2000-2021

This chart supports Bengen's assertion that small-cap stocks returned more to investors than large-cap stocks over 20 years. This small asset class delivered superior returns, and because they didn't have a perfect correlation to large-cap stocks they diversified the portfolio. $10,000 increased to more than $66,131 in the small-cap index fund and $39,799 in the large-cap index fund. I used two mutual funds for this chart because comparable ETFs did not exist 20 years ago.

- Portfolio 1 - NAESX $10,000 $66,131 9.30%
- Portfolio 2 - VFINX $10,000 $39,799 6.72%

The "take-away" lesson is that small-cap ETFs may outperform over long periods, and they will diversify a portfolio that's heavily weighted toward large-cap companies.

I have found that it's easy to own more large-cap funds or stocks because the S&P 500 index is dominated mainly by large tech companies. Any investor in the US who owns stocks or funds may already own shares in these large-cap companies. If you're just starting you are in a good position to capture the returns of different asset classes by diversifying your portfolio early on.

61

Nobel Prize laureate Harry Markowitz said, "Diversification is the only free lunch" in investing, and the addition of small-cap stocks to a portfolio is a good example of what he was talking about.[16] By investing in small cap stocks, an investor can potentially improve total returns and can certainly diversify a portfolio that's heavily weighted toward large-cap stocks.

Small-cap ETF summary

Small-cap ETFs focus on companies that are not represented in large cap index funds and ETFs like the S&P 500 that are popular with many investors. During the past decade small cap stocks have underperformed large caps, but over a 20 year time period small cap stocks outperformed large caps.

This small asset class provides diversification for investors with portfolios dominated by large-cap stocks. They provide this exposure to a large swath of stocks in the small-cap universe at very low cost.

12

SMALL-CAP VALUE ETFS

Small-cap value ETFs have lagged the overall market for several years, as large-cap stocks have dominated market returns. Within the universe of smaller companies, we can see that over the past decade growth stocks have performed better than value.

Value stocks have been stuck in the doldrums more than 10 years; regardless of whether a company is large or small, domestic or international, almost all value stocks have performed poorly compared to growth.

Investors have been attracted to growth stocks and are willing to pay higher and higher prices for them. They are excited about money a company make earn in the future, even if current earnings are trivial or nonexistent. There is *low demand for companies with consistent profits*, and high demand for companies seen as driving innovation in the future.

My portfolio is *tilted* toward value stocks, meaning I have more exposure to these low-valuation stocks. It can be frustrating to see my investments *go nowhere for years,* and I often think of selling those mutual funds and putting the money elsewhere. I know as soon as I do that...*value will roar back*!

This value tilt exists because several years ago I invested in global and international *mutual funds* run by Dodge & Cox, a value investing fund company with a history as successful value investors. Because I don't sell investments very often, I've held those investments through thick and thin. *It is not easy* to hold stocks that go nowhere for years, but it's also no fun to switch boats midstream because it's impossible to time the market with any consistency. I believe that over many years, well-run companies with earnings will deliver good returns to investors, so I'm holding.

> Many shall be restored that now are fallen and many shall fall that now are in honor.
>
> — Horace

Horace's observation is a good reminder that today's growth stocks shall one day fall, and value, now fallen, shall be restored.

In the late 2020, and in early 2021 as I write this, value stocks seem to be staging a comeback. *Maybe value investing is not dead after all.* If you think about it rationally, *if you knew growth stocks would always outperform,* value stocks would have no purpose at all and you could just invest in growth stocks. But, investors like real earnings they can count on, and when they start to crave money today over expected money in the future, value tends to shine.

Those who invest in S&P 500 index funds today invest heavily in growth whether they like it or not. This is because the stocks that dominate that index are growth stocks like Apple, Microsoft, Amazon, Facebook, Google, and Tesla, the largest holdings in the S&P 500 as of this writing.[1] So, if investors don't want this heavy growth tilt they have to find a way to balance this out, and this is where value ETFs could help to diversify a growth-heavy portfolio.

Small-cap value stocks

Small-cap value stocks represent the smallest, lowest-valuation stocks in the market. This means their prices are low compared to their earnings or book value. You could consider small-cap value stocks as being at the opposite end of the size and valuation spectrum from large-cap growth stocks.

Fama and French, the academics mentioned earlier, wrote in their landmark 2014 paper that, "The new model shows that the highest expected returns are attained by companies that are small, profitable and value companies with no major growth prospects."[2]

I have no reason to believe that academics are better investors than anyone else. I think the key concepts of intelligent investing are simple can be learned without a college education or exposure to academic theories.

However, I like to learn and part of that is consuming new information that may or may not be useful. I like to ask questions and dig to see whether a new idea makes sense. You'll recall that at the beginning of this book I wrote, "I'm perceptive when it comes to noticing details around me, and that helps as a photographer. Strong skills of perception also help me focus on what matters as an investor." Well, examining small cap-value is just such an instance of leaving no stone unturned and seeing where I can find something useful to share with readers.

If Fama and French are correct, then over the long term, *small value stocks will return more than large, growth stocks.* My first question is whether you would have been better off during the past 10 years owning large-cap growth stocks or small-cap value stocks. To answer this question I used portfolio visualizer to make the chart below comparing a small-cap value ETF with the S&P 500 index ETF.[3] The large cap S&P 500 contains a mixture of both growth and value stocks.

10 Year Experiment: Small-Cap Value vs. S&P 500

Portfolio | Initial Balance | Final Balance | CAGR

- Portfolio 1 - Small-cap value index $10,000 $32,015 11.82%
- Portfolio 2 - S&P 500 index $10,000 $40,734 14.43%

For this comparison I used the Vanguard Small-Cap Value Index Fund (VISVX) and the Vanguard S&P 500 Index fund because the corresponding ETFs did not exist 20 years ago. The returns, however, should be virtually the same as those of the corresponding ETFs.

So, you can see that both funds performed similarly until about 2019, and the value fund lagged as the S&P 500 fund surged up. The difference is a significant 2.4% which amounted to an extra $8,800 for the S&P fund.

Anyone who has invested during the past 10 years knows which fund won. But how about returns over the past 20 years?

20 Year Experiment: Small-Cap Value vs. S&P 500

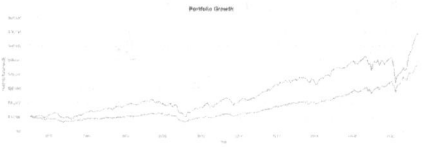

Portfolio | Initial Balance | Final Balance | CAGR

- Portfolio 1 - Small-Cap Value Index $10,000 $68,780 9.91%

- Portfolio 2 - S&P 500 Index $10,000 $46,406 7.81%

What a difference the longer timeframe makes! The small-cap value fund trounced the large-cap S&P 500 fund and *generated $25,000 in excess returns* over the 20 year period. During its best year, the small-cap value fund gained 37.19% while in its best year the S&P 500 it gained 32.18%. During its worst year, the small-cap value fund returned -32.05%, and the S&P 500 returned -37.02%.

In other words, the small-cap value fund *gained more in its best year* and *lost less in its worse year* while leaving the investor with a lot more money in the end: $68,780 vs $46,408.

Nobody can predict what will happen in the future. If stock returns in the future are similar to those in the past, then small-cap value ETFs make sense. However, markets are constantly changing and there is not certainty that an asset class that outperformed for twenty years in the past will continue to deliver excess return in the future.

While there are no guarantees for investors, there are three observations in favor of small-cap funds compared S&P 500 index funds. During the 20-year period between 2000 to 2020, the small cap value fund:

1. Gained more in up years
2. Lost less in down years
3. Provided excess returns

I have not invested in a small-cap value fund yet because it was only recently that I came across Fama and French's paper. However, I did invest in the Vanguard Small-Cap ETF (VB) during the stock market crash in March of 2020 to gain small-cap exposure to balance the my S&P 500 ETF which provides no exposure to small-cap stocks.

I am curious how a small-cap *value* ETF like IJS compares to a small-cap blend ETF like VB (which holds both growth and value stocks).

I decided to use portfolio visualizer to compare both ETFs, and I used the Vanguard small-cap index fund NAESX instead of VB, which did not exist 20 years ago. This seems like an "apples to apples" substitution because both NAESX and VB have identical objectives.

In a comparison of 20 years of performance between small-cap *value* EFT and small-cap blend, value narrowly edged out blend 10.03% to 9.92% — a *minuscule* .1% over a long time frame.

Since small cap ETFs *include* value stocks found in a small value fund, I see no need to invest in small-cap value specifically unless an investor *really wants to have a small-cap value "pure play"* ETF in their portfolio.

Three Small-Cap Value ETFs

You will see the three largest small-cap value ETFs featured below. As soon as I made a graph to compare their results I could see that their long-term returns were *identical*. These ETFs charge an expense ratio of .15% or .18%, and this expense does not seem to affect returns.

If you prefer to own the lowest expense funds possible, then you might favor VIOV or SLYV, but IJS has existed longer than the other two ETFs and is more frequently traded, which could result in lower trading spreads.[4]

iShares S&P SmallCap 600 Value ETF (IJS)

Top 15 Holdings
    Expense ratio: .18%
    Symbol / Holding / % Assets

1. BlackRock Cash Funds Treasury SL Agency Shares 1.94%
2. M Macy's Inc 0.90%
3. GME GameStop Corp. Class A 0.88%
4. REZI Resideo Technologies, Inc. 0.75%
5. ABG Asbury Automotive Group, Inc. 0.74%
6. PPBI Pacific Premier Bancorp, Inc. 0.70%

THE ETF INVESTOR

7. BKU BankUnited, Inc. 0.69%
8. PDCE PDC Energy, Inc. 0.66%
9. FHB First Hawaiian, Inc. 0.65%
10. ABM ABM Industries Incorporated 0.65%
11. NSIT Insight Enterprises, Inc. 0.64%
12. SIG Signet Jewelers Limited 0.62%
13. AVA Avista Corporation 0.60%
14. ABCB Ameris Bancorp 0.59%
15. ONB Old National Bancorp 0.54%

Number of Holdings: 475
% of Assets in Top 15: 8.56%

Vanguard S&P Small-Cap 600 Value ETF (VIOV)

Top 15 Holdings
Expense ratio: .15%
Symbol / Company / % Assets

1. M Macy's Inc. 0.92%
2. U.S. Dollar 0.86%
3. PPBI Pacific Premier Bancorp, Inc. 0.74%
4. BKU BankUnited, Inc. 0.73%
5. FHB First Hawaiian, Inc. 0.71%
6. AGO Assured Guaranty Ltd. 0.70%
7. PDCE PDC Energy, Inc. 0.68%
8. BBBY Bed Bath & Beyond Inc. 0.66%
9. REZI Resideo Technologies, Inc. 0.66%
10. ABCB Ameris Bancorp 0.65%
11. ABG Asbury Automotive Group, Inc. 0.64%
12. COLB Columbia Banking System, Inc. 0.62%
13. SFNC Simmons First National Corporation Class A 0.62%
14. HP Helmerich & Payne, Inc. 0.60%
15. ONB Old National Bancorp 0.59%

Number of Holdings: 473
% of Assets in Top 15: 7.71%

SPDR S&P 600 Small Cap Value ETF (SLYV)

SLYV seeks to replicate the same small cap value benchmark as the two other ETFs mentioned above.

Top 15 Holdings

Expense ratio: .15%

Symbol / Company / % Assets

1. M Macy's Inc. 0.95%
2. GME GameStop Corp. Class A 0.84%
3. REZI Resideo Technologies, Inc. 0.76%
4. BKU BankUnited, Inc. 0.73%
5. ABG Asbury Automotive Group, Inc. 0.73%
6. PPBI Pacific Premier Bancorp, Inc. 0.72%
7. FHB First Hawaiian, Inc. 0.65%
8. NSIT Insight Enterprises, Inc. 0.65%
9. ABM ABM Industries Incorporated 0.64%
10. AGO Assured Guaranty Ltd. 0.64%
11. ABCB Ameris Bancorp 0.63%
12. ISBC Investors Bancorp Inc 0.61%
13. PDCE PDC Energy, Inc. 0.61%
14. AVA Avista Corporation 0.60%
15. ONB Old National Bancorp 0.58%

Number of Holdings: 474
% of Assets in Top 15: 7.31%

The long-term returns for all three funds are practically identical: 12.27% for IJS, 12.19% for VIOV, and 12.32% for SLYV. As you can see, the three funds are mirror-images of one another, and I provide these three options so you can see for yourself. If you look at the holdings you will see a lot of overlap in the stocks they hold.

As I explained earlier, I saw no excess returns when comparing small cap *blend* ETFs and small-cap *value* ETFs. Because both of these small-cap funds exhibit identical long-term performance, I see the big difference existing between small-cap and large-cap ETFs. I believe the question is less about which is the perfect small-cap fund, and more about whether to invest in small-caps ETFs.

Actively-Managed Small Cap Value ETF

Another option for those who may want to invest in small-cap value ETFs is Avantis U.S. Small-Cap Value ETF (AVUV), an *actively-managed* small-cap value ETF. While this fund does not have a long track record, it's worth keeping on your radar because its managers have a mandate to actively select stocks when economic developments suggest that stock picking could provide returns in excess of a passively managed index fund.

AVUV's returns could potentially diverge from the small-cap value indexes mentioned earlier in this chapter because fund managers have the ability to make investment decisions based on stock prices or their opinions about the economy.

Avantis U.S. Small Cap Value ETF (AVUV)

The fund invests in a diverse group of small-cap value companies it expects to generate higher returns.

Top 15 Holdings

Expense ratio: .25%

Symbol / Company / % Assets

1. LPX Louisiana-Pacific Corp 0.95%
2. XEC Cimarex Energy Co 0.84%
3. TRGP Targa Resources Corp 0.76%
4. AN AutoNation Inc 0.73%
5. OVV Ovintiv Inc 0.73%
6. AA Alcoa Corp 0.72%
7. SF Stifel Financial Corp 0.65%
8. M Macy's Inc 0.65%
9. FL Foot Locker Inc 0.64%
10. SAKA Saia Inc 0.64%

Number of Holdings: 570

% of Assets in Top 10: 7.55%

According to Morningstar, "Management on the team is unseasoned; the longest-tenured manager on the team, Ted Randall, has only about one year of industry experience."[5]

I would not be concerned on the short tenure of fund management. The other ETFs in this category are index funds, and their managers don't jump in or out of holdings, but make small adjustments to track their respective indexes.

An investor in AVUV would presumably desire active portfolio management, and when it comes to an active manager, their decisions are likely to be bad as good, and the results will likely diverge from the index, which is what an investor wants — otherwise they can own the index at lower cost. It's obvious that an investor would want to beat the index by investing in an actively managed ETF, but a realist should expect not only divergent returns compared to the index ETF, but also realize the fund might just as likely do worse than the index as do better.

The fund company's website states, "AVUV pursues the benefits associated with indexing (diversification, low turnover, transparency of exposures), but with the ability to add value by making investment decisions using information in current prices."[6] It should be noted that the company cannot promise to achieve their objectives.

Small-cap value stocks are not as closely followed by Wall Street analysts because of these companies' sizes. Because of this, it may be likely that this group of stocks could be underpriced compared to those of larger companies. If this is true, a non-indexed ETF like AVUV may have a better chance outperforming small value index funds if the fund mangers meet their objectives.

Given that large companies have grown so rapidly and their stock valuations seem high by many estimates, a rational investor could invest in small-cap value ETFs to diversify a portfolio that might be weighted toward large cap growth stocks.

In Search of Ultra-Small Companies

We've been looking at small-cap stocks, but there is a category of stocks that invests in even *tinier* companies. I'm on a quest to find an ETF that holds ultra-small stocks because I know of a *mutual fund* that holds only ultra-small cap stocks. Bridgeway Ultra-Small Company (BRSIX) *buys only the smallest 10% of the small-cap stocks in the CRSP US Small Cap Index.* I owned shares in this fund for years until I sold them to buy a house.

I've been thinking about buying back in to this unique asset class ever since I lost the ultra-small cap stock exposure when I bought the house because after selling that fund my portfolio became large-cap dominated. Large-caps have performed well, but every now and then I think that it would be good to regain ultra-small cap exposure again. But where can I buy an ETF that holds such small companies?

One of the rare things about Bridgeway's fund is that *ultra-small company* stocks have a weighted average market cap of only $258 million. *These are the tiniest of the small-cap companies*, and many of which make only one product or service. That makes ultra-small cap stocks vulnerable to steep declines in bear markets, but causes them to shoot up in bull markets and economic recoveries.

Compare the weighted average market cap of $3.7 billion for Vanguard's Small-Cap VB with $258 million for Bridgeway's Ultra Small-Company (BRSIX). The Vanguard ETF's stocks are 14x larger than the Bridgeway mutual fund, whose stocks are an order of magnitude smaller.

I have never been able to find and ETF like BRSIX. The Fund aims to approximate the total return of the Cap-Based Portfolio 10 Index published by the University of Chicago's Center for Research in Security Prices (CRSP) over long time periods. "Ultra-small companies" are defined as those companies that have a market capitalization the size of the smallest 10% of companies listed on the New York Stock Exchange, or companies with capitalizations that fall within the range of companies included in the CRSP 10 Index.[7]

It has been difficult to find any ETFs that invest in "ultra-small companies." These companies are so small many of them sell just one product or service. For investors who want exposure to small-cap value stocks like those discussed by Fama and French's, it may be interesting to note the ultra small-cap companies in the BRSIX portfolio skew *toward the value end* of the small cap spectrum.

Now, I had almost convinced myself of the futility of finding an ETF equivalent for the Bridgeway Ultra-Small Company Fund — but I never gave up despite finding this discouraging notice while searching for on ETF Database:

> "We're sorry, there are no active ETFs associated with this index."
>
> — ETF DATABASE

I did not let that discourage me; I kept on digging, and one evening while elbows deep in data, a sparkling nugget appeared: an ETF called RWJ.

Invesco S&P SmallCap 600 Revenue ETF (RWJ)

I found this ETFs during a bizarre search in which I decided to find funds with the highest year-to-date returns from January through April 29, 2021. You may ask why I was looking for high returning ETFs, the here was my reasoning: since *small-caps* had outpaced large-caps all year, and *value stocks* outpaced growth, the best performing ETFs would probably hold the *small value stocks*.

RWJ most likely had phenomenal returns because of its unique methodology. It invests in small companies with growing revenues. It was not an ultra-small company fund — its average market cap is $2.3 billion which lands it in the small-cap category.

This ETF fishes from a value pond with a plan to catch value fish that increases revenues rapidly. When it reviews its catch, there are many *small value stocks* in the net. Although the objective of the fund

THE ETF INVESTOR

is to invest in stocks with growing revenues, the chart below shows its holdings fall into the "small" and "value" categories.

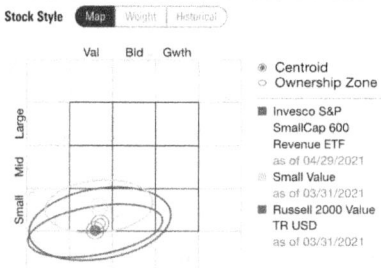

Invesco S&P SmallCap 600 Revenue ETF (RWJ) has a portfolio of smaller, value-oriented companies compared with its average peer. Source: Morningstar ETF report, April 30, 2021

RWJ tracks an index of S&P SmallCap 600 Index stocks that are weighted by revenue. This is interesting is one of a handful of small-cap ETFs that use a fundamentals-weighted methodology. It selects stocks for its portfolio based on top-line revenue instead of market-cap. The fund mechanically buys positive revenue-producing securities of the S&P SmallCap 600, and that index defines a constituent's revenue by the sum of its most recently reported trailing four-quarter revenues.[8]

I thought the best performing small cap value stocks would hold the tiniest stocks, but I found small cap value stocks with *positive revenues*.

What sets this apart?

Investors who might want to include small-cap ETFs in their long-term portfolios using a unique weighting methodology.

Many ETFs, like those listed at the beginning of this chapter, use *market cap-weighting*. The problem with this approach is that the index owns more large companies and fewer small companies. This strategy tends to skew the portfolio towards overvalued stocks.

RWJ's approach may appeal to investors who want to shift their small-cap exposure toward companies with low price-to-sales multiples, and it appeals to investors who prefer alternatives to market cap-weighting to avoid the strategy's tendency to skew towards overvalued stocks.

To provide you with more analysis behind the ETF's methodology, this fund company's website describes the fund's objective this way: "RWJ seeks to track the investment results of the S&P SmallCap 600, a market-cap-weighted index that consists of US small-cap companies screened for size, liquidity, and financial viability." This fund uses the sum of companies' most *recently reported trailing four-quarter revenues* as the basis for inclusion; those with the highest revenues are more heavily weighted.[9]

RWJ uses a unique methodology that looks at money flowing into the company instead of mechanically buying companies based on average market weighting. I think it's a worthwhile ETF to consider for small-cap value exposure (or simply as a way to gain small-cap fund exposure) especially because its .39% expense ratio gives it a sizable cost advantage over many "factor investing" competitors as RWJ expenses are within the lowest fee quintile among peers.[10]

As a side note, I would not pay an ETF expense ratio greater than .50% because you can gain exposure to almost any asset class at the low expense of .03% to .18%. If an investor pays much more in annual expenses they should get return in excess of that ongoing fee, but unfortunately there's no guarantee that paying more in expenses will yield better results.

Also, 1% in fees (or anything close to it) can really add up over time. In 10 or 20 years, depending on how much you've invested, it could cost you $10,000 or $20,000 in money that could be going to you, but instead gets handed to the fund's manager. Wall Street is designed to extract fees from you to pay their managers' salaries. So, even a fee of .65% or .75% for an actively managed ETF can be costly in the long run if the fund isn't providing returns in excess of what you could get for .03% or .05%.

I point this out simply because I think many investors give up more than necessary without realizing it, and I think people should know that with so many options, paying .50% or more in annual expenses seems steep.

Don't get me wrong: if you could guarantee a higher expense ratio would give you better returns you would pay that fee *all day long*. But I think what happens is that hot performance attracts investors who ignore the high fee because the return is so great, but eventually the astronomic returns disappear while the expenses remain.

I favor cheap ETFs because you keep more of the market's return and pay less to the fund manager, but I have no problem making exceptions and believe that paying .39% for RWJ seems reasonable.

Also, I would go into any ETF investment thinking that *it might wind up not working out*. If that's the case and the fund doesn't outperform small cap category, I'm still getting exposure to the asset class at a reasonable expense.

If it turned out to be a real stinker, there would be no reason not to sell shares and buy into a small cap ETF with extremely low costs.

One more graph

I made this graph for you, my reader, because this graph shows you that just because a few different ETFs are named "small value" that does not mean they invest in the same kinds of stocks or their returns will be the same.

As an example, let's take a look small-cap value RWJ, which we just looked at, as well as SLYV and IJS, two small-cap value ETFs we discussed earlier in the chapter.

RWJ is Portfolio 1 (top) SLYV is Portfolio 2 (middle) and IJS is Portfolio 3 (bottom).

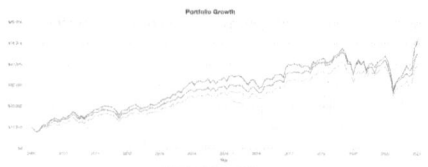

This graph shows three "small-cap value" ETFs that all behaved similarly over the course of 12 years. However, even though they moved in tandem, Portfolio 1 (RWJ) generated a greater total return than the two other funds. Most of this return seems to have been generated during the most recent few months of 2021 as RWJ delivered a 42.82% return from January through April.

I'm not going to go into all the holdings, because they're beside the point here. I want you to see these ETF's returns from 2009 to 2021.

Portfolio | Initial Balance | Final Balance | CAGR

- Portfolio 1 - RWJ $10,000 $50,775 14.50%
- Portfolio 2 - SLYV $10,000 $45,172 13.39%
- Portfolio 3 - IJS $10,000 $40,173 12.29%

As you can see, all three small-cap value ETFs performed differently. RWJ generated $5,000 more than SLYV, and $10,000 more than IJS, and it was the clear winner in this comparison.

What I notice more than anything is that all three funds behaved similarly during the period, with RWJ slightly outperforming the others for much of the decade. Its superior performance is mainly due to rocketing up at the beginning of 2021 — as it generated a 42.82% YTD return in just four months.[11]

I think the take-home lesson here is that you might just do well and turn your $10,000 into $40,000 in about 12 years, which would be an excellent result. If you get luck on your side, there's always a chance that you get a fund like RWJ that adds an extra $10,000 to your total and you end up with a $50,000 return.

Having seen how much of a bonus you can get being in the

perfect ETF, I'd like to let you know that even though that's a human desire — and I applaud you for wanting to maximize your gains — just remember that you can't control your returns. You can control your costs — and all three of these ETFs have reasonable expenses below .40%.

Yet, it's impossible to predict which fund will "beat" others other funds in a given category. Instead, I think it's better for your mental balance to deal with something within your control: ask yourself whether you might want to diversify your portfolio, and gain exposure to an asset class that historically provides returns in excess of the total stock market over long periods.

Small-Cap Value ETF summary

Small-cap *value* ETFs focus on companies that have lower valuations compared to the small cap ETFs discussed in the prior chapter.

In other words, these are the *lowest valuation small-cap stocks* within the small-company universe. Academic research shows that over long periods of time (20 years or more) *small-value stocks outperformed* large cap funds like the S&P 500 funds and ETFs popular with many investors.

The comparison and graph presented above confirms the academic findings of small value superiority during the period between 2000 and 2020, however there is no way to know if this advantage will persist.

13

MEGA-CAP GROWTH ETF

What is larger and faster-growing than the S&P 500? Well, that would be a "Mega Cap Growth" ETF that focuses exclusively on the largest, fastest-growing companies in the US. That fund is Vanguard Mega Cap Growth ETF.

Vanguard Mega-Cap Growth ETF (MGK)

This ETF provides an enormous contrast to the small-cap offerings discussed earlier. This fund invests only in the largest growth companies in the US.

This is a concentrated fund. While some of the small-cap ETFs we looked at in the last chapter own more than 1,000 stocks, this is a different beast, holding only 112 stocks with 59% of the fund invested in the top 15 holdings[1].

MGK invests in the largest fast-growing companies in the US that represent the most richly valued half of the large-cap stock universe. As an interesting side note, this ETF held up well during the pandemic. The strength of mega-cap stocks in MGK's portfolio is obvious: in midst of the pandemic in May of 2020 before a vaccine had been distributed, this ETF had a YTD return of +.26%.[2] During the same time the S&P 500 index generated a return of -10.31%[3]. Mega-cap stocks provided resiliency and positive returns during this period of extreme pessimism and uncertainty.

Vanguard Mega Cap Growth Index Fund ETF Shares (MGK)

Top 15 Holdings[4]
Expense ratio: .07%
Symbol / Holding / % Assets

1. MSFT Microsoft Corp 12.07%
2. AAPL Apple Inc 10.48%
3. AMZN Amazon.com Inc 8.75%
4. FB Facebook Inc 4.41%
5. GOOGL Alphabet Inc 3.56%
6. GOOG Alphabet Inc 3.49%
7. V Visa Inc 2.72%
8. MA Mastercard Inc 2.19%
9. HD Home Depot Inc 2.16%
10. NFLX Netflix Inc 1.65%
11. CMCSA Comcast Corp 1.52%
12. ADBE Adobe Inc 1.51%
13. NVDA NVIDIA Corp 1.49%
14. PYPL PayPal Holdings Inc 1.28%
15. MCD Mcdonald's Corp 1.25%

Number of Holdings: 112
% of Assets in Top 15: 58.95%

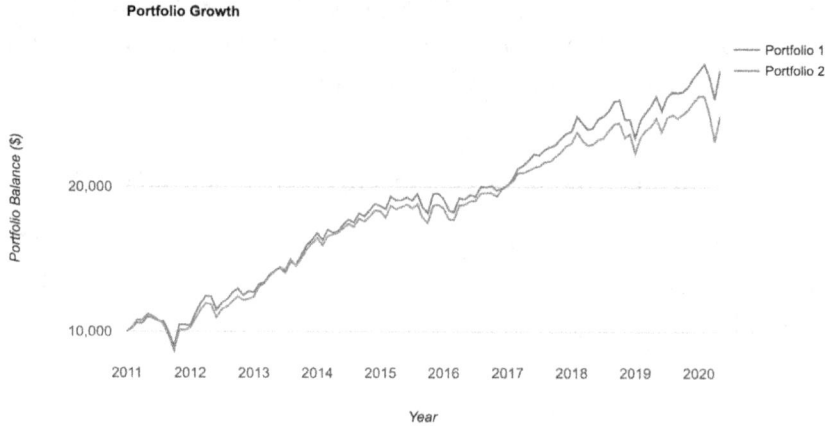

MGK (top) vs VOO over 12 year period. Source: Portfolio Visualizer. May 14, 2020

You can see that during the past 12 years the largest of the large-caps — the "mega-caps" have dominated stock market returns. Whether this outperformance will continue for the next decade is anyone's guess.

Investors who want to invest in a diversified large-cap ETF that focuses on the 100 largest companies in the S&P 500 might find this fund useful.

During this time of investor uncertainty, these large growth companies have drawn strong investor interest. One sector of the economy that has been especially strong is tech companies, which typically have a low cost of capital, are scalable, and are capable of growing their businesses in a remote-working environment.

Beginning investors should know that strong performance in one sector of the stock market (like growth companies) *does not always persist*. There are no guarantees that the companies that have performed well during the past several years will dominate future returns.

From the mid 1990s through 2000, the stock prices of tech and Internet stocks rocketed to breathtaking heights. Everyone who owned them or mutual funds that held them saw their portfolios balloon. This fever for these high growth sectors lasted for about 5 years, and then they crashed suddenly, dealing a financial blow to investors. I point this out because often the "sure thing" with all investors can change unexpectedly, and today's hot stock is often tomorrow's cheap stock.

It makes sense to do a "reality check" periodically to make sure you are not betting too heavily that the current situation will persist. The mega-cap growth category described above has done well over the past decade, but there is no guarantee about the next several years; be prepared for chaos and the possibility that these stocks may fall from favor.

Growth stocks have dominated markets from 2010 to 2020. It's hard to know if growth will continue to beat value for a long time, or value stocks will once again have their day in the sun.

Keep in mind that no ETF guarantees success in every environment.

Mega-Cap Growth ETF Summary

A Mega-cap growth ETF is a bet on large-cap growth stocks to dominate the future as they have in the past. This approach might appeal to investors who want to "tilt" their portfolio toward this sector, and may be suitable for those who want to make a focused mega-cap growth investment without owning many other asset classes found in a diversified ETF.

14

MID-CAP ETFS

Until now we have focused on ETFs that invest in small-cap and large-cap stocks. Mid-caps ETFs invest in stocks that might remind some people of Goldilocks: *"Not too big and not too small."* These companies fit in size-wise between the babies and giants of the investing world; you can think of them as teenagers.

Mid-cap (or mid-capitalization) describes companies with a market cap —or market value—between $2 and $10 billion. Classifications like large-cap, mid-cap, and small-cap are approximations of company value, and the stocks in these indexes change over time.[1]

This category is often overlooked by investors because the companies represented are not yet the enormous growth powerhouses that drive the economy. However, many of these companies like Lululemon, Moderna, and Pinterest are not unknown startups either. Many of these companies are in that transitional teenage phase; they've outgrown their small-cap status, yet they're not in the big leagues yet.

I've noticed that mid-cap stock returns fall somewhere between those of large-cap and small-cap stocks, and I think that may be the reason they get skipped over in conversations about stocks and asset allocation decisions: people seem to pick either large-cap or small-cap stocks. Still, the fast-growing stocks in these ETFs might make sense for investors who don't want the volatility of small-cap ETFs, but don't want to own companies like Alphabet, Apple, Bank of America, Facebook, Walmart, and other behemoths of the large cap world that are *already enormous* and less likely to grow as rapidly as some of the companies in this ETF.

As you review the three funds that follow you will see the first ETF is labeled "growth," the second "blend" (a mixture of growth and value), and the last "value." To provide a quick summary: growth stocks often have higher valuations, and could be considered *expensive*, while value stocks have lower valuations, and could be considered *cheap*. Blend is a mixture of growth and value. I think it's worth pointing out that it's not necessarily bad that growth stocks are expensive — this may be the case because investors anticipate strong future growth.

Along those lines, it's not necessarily a benefit that value stocks are cheap: investors might think the companies are not growing fast enough or have fallen out of favor. The one thing you should keep in mind is that valuation tells you something, *but not everything*, about a company. Investor emotions can drive stock prices and make stocks trend higher or lower, and investors often exhibit crowd-like behavior. So, keep in mind "expensive" and "cheap" are broad and non-specific terms that help ETFs determine which stocks make the list of holdings, but these labels don't tell us much about which styles will prevail in the future.

You may have noticed that sometimes growth stocks outperform value stocks, and sometimes it's the other way around. Remember that no investing style succeeds in all seasons, and the current trend (whether it favors growth or value) will probably not last forever. One thing I find interesting about small-cap and mid-cap ETFs is that the companies within these portfolios seem to change frequently, an indication of the rapid growth of successful companies and decline of others.

The constant change of stocks in these indexes reflects the competitive forces in business, and ways that the strong survive and force out the weak. One interesting aspect of mid-cap ETFs is that like their small-cap counterparts, they are often filled with the rapidly growing companies that will grow to become the future's successful large stocks. This is an investor's chance to buy the fast growers while they are relative unknowns before they hit the big time.

For example, the largest position in this fund, Moderna (MRNA) was not a top 15 holding in the spring of 2020. Yet one year later, in 2021 the company is a household name and may one day become a well-known large cap drug company. This rapid ascent from an unknown small-cap to superstar stock shows the rapid growth potential of mid-cap growth stocks. If Moderna continues its ascent it will not be long before it is a large-cap growth stock. Investors in this ETF would benefit from its success without the risk of having to put all their eggs in the Moderna basket.

iShares Morningstar Mid-Cap Growth ETF (IMCG)

Top 15 Holdings[2]
Expense ratio: .06%
Symbol / Holding / % Assets

1. MRNA Moderna, Inc.1.23%
2. CRWD CrowdStrike Holdings, Inc. Class A0.96%
3. INFO IHS Markit Ltd.0.94%
4. MTCH Match Group, Inc.0.93%
5. MSCI MSCI Inc. Class A0.92%
6. ROKU Roku, Inc. Class A0.92%
7. MRVL Marvell Technology, Inc.0.91%
8. CDNS Cadence Design Systems, Inc.0.85%
9. PANW Palo Alto Networks, Inc.0.85%
10. DXCM DexCom, Inc.0.81%
11. PINS Pinterest, Inc. Class A0.81%
12. FRC First Republic Bank0.79%
13. AME AMETEK, Inc.0.73%
14. FAST Fastenal Company0.72%

15. RMD ResMed Inc. 0.72%

One thing you'll notice just taking a look at this *growth* ETF is that it features many companies in the biotech, and tech sectors. Moderna, which developed the Covid-19 vaccine, is a rapidly growing biotech company, DexCom makes glucose monitoring systems, Roku manufactures digital media players for video streaming, and Palo Alto Networks is a cybersecurity company. Just a year ago, payment processor Square was a top holding in this ETF, and its rapid growth to a $93 billion market-cap has moved it into large-cap ETFs. Those who own mid-cap ETFs benefit from fast growers like Moderna and Square.

Next, let's take a look at a mid-cap "blend" fund that owns a mixture of fast-growing and high valuation "growth" stocks and cheap "value" stocks.

Vanguard Mid-Cap Index ETF (VO)

Top 15 Holdings[3]
Expense ratio: .04%
Symbol / Holding / % Assets

1. IDXX IDEXX Laboratories, Inc. 0.70%
2. IQV IQVIA Holdings Inc. 0.68%
3. DLR Digital Realty Trust, Inc. 0.65%
4. CMG Chipotle Mexican Grill, Inc. 0.63%
5. APH Amphenol Corporation Class A 0.61%
6. MCHP Microchip Technology Incorporated 0.61%
7. DOCU DocuSign, Inc. 0.59%
8. MTCH Match Group, Inc. 0.58%
9. INFO IHS Markit Ltd. 0.58%
10. APTV Aptiv PLC 0.58%
11. VEEV Veeva Systems Inc Class A 0.58%
12. SNPS Synopsys, Inc. 0.57%
13. MSCI MSCI Inc. Class A 0.57%

14. CARR Carrier Global Corp. 0.57%
15. SNPS Synopsys Inc. 0.56%

You can see that this portfolio is a mid-cap *blend* which means it owns some growth stocks like Markit, Match Group, and MSCI (all three stocks included in the IMCG portfolio discussed earlier) as well as cheaper *value* stocks like Clorox and Newmont Corporation.

Let's take a look at another ETF that focuses only on mid-cap *value* stocks. These are the stocks that a variety of metrics suggest are selling cheaply compared to other mid-cap stocks.

Invesco S&P MidCap 400® Pure Value ETF (RFV)

Top 15 Holdings[4]
 Expense ratio: .35%
 Symbol / Holding / % Assets

1. TDS Telephone and Data Systems, Inc. 2.43%
2. AVT Avnet, Inc. 2.28%
3. CMC Commercial Metals Co. 2.01%
4. NAVI Navient Corp. 1.94%
5. AN AutoNation, Inc. 1.88%
6. KSS Kohl's Corp. 1.83%
7. GHC Graham Holdings Co. 1.82%
8. SNX SYNNEX Corp. 1.79%
9. INT World Fuel Services Corp. 1.74%
10. XRX Xerox Holdings Corp. 1.69%
11. ARW Arrow Electronics, Inc. 1.66%
12. TMHC Taylor Morrison Home Corp. 1.59%
13. RGA Reinsurance Group of America, Inc. 1.59%
14. DAN Dana Inc. 1.57%
15. TPH Tri Pointe Homes, Inc. 1.54%

The stocks in RFV have lower valuations relative to the stocks in the other mid-cap ETFs. These stocks' prices are low relative to their earnings because their holdings are in less demand or out of favor with investors for some reason(s). Because these stocks are somewhat "unloved," their valuations and stock prices are low compared to other stocks in the mid-cap stock universe.

Does that mean those who invest in this ETF are getting bargains? It's hard to say, and I can tell you from personal experience that when value stocks are performing horribly it's hard to get excited about them, especially when you see some other asset class soaring to new heights. However, with experience an investor learns that sometimes today's unloved companies can suddenly come into favor. When demand for value stocks reappears, the benefits of owning cheap and unloved stocks suddenly becomes obvious.

Remember that *a low stock price does not indicate a bad or unprofitable company*. Sometimes low prices occur when *perfectly good companies are overlooked by investors* who are momentarily distracted by some other bright and shiny investments. Investors tend to dump their boring and predictable companies in favor of the flavor of the moment, and these emotional decisions can cause the stocks of wonderful companies to sell at cheap prices.

Part of intelligent investment happens when you realize that companies that are out of favor can suddenly come in strong demand for their consistent cash flows and profitability. During 2020 the stocks of profitable companies became cheap as investors during the Covid-19 pandemic sold stocks in companies that would likely suffer with customers stuck at home.

In this environment, tech companies like Amazon, Apple, Docusign, eBay, Facebook, Fedex, Moderna, Nvidia, PayPal, and Zoom had the greatest stock price appreciation as people worked remotely and scaled back their use of oil, dined out less, traveled less, and postponed vacations.

Stocks that depended on customers shopping at malls, going to work, and traveling became the cheap "value" stocks as their prices declined Simon Property Group, Carnival Corp., Delta Air Lines, SL Green Realty Corp., United Airlines, Norwegian Cruise Lines and Southwest Airlines became cheap "value" stocks and their prices fell from -38% to -58% due to fears related to their future survival and profitability.⁵

It makes sense for you, as an ETF investor, to realize that different investing styles can shine brightly at different times, just as different trees or plants have blossoms and give fruit in different seasons. You can't expect everything to be in bloom at the same time, and for this very reason it makes sense to spread out your investments to capture returns of different asset classes.

The ETFs in this chapter — as well as the others discussed in this book can smooth out the bumps in the long-term investors drive and help *generate excellent long-term investment results*, even if they're not popular with other investors, or "in bloom" right now. Keep these different asset classes in mind as a way to diversify your portfolio, especially if your portfolio is already weighted toward large stocks or growth stocks.⁶

When people get fearful in markets, they either bail out and sell their stocks, or they buy stocks that are going up. People tend to jump in and out of stocks and focus on short-term trends, which means they often ignore perfectly good companies they deem non-essential or vulnerable.

If you look at the graph below, you'll see IMCG (growth) on top, then VO (blend) in the middle, and then RFV (value) at the bottom during the decade leading up to the pandemic, with the sudden drop occurring in March of 2020.

It would be perfectly understandable if a reader took the "short cut" and decided to avoid value RFV (the bottom line) because it dropped farthest during the corona crash. I understand wanting to avoid the laggard, but keep in mind that these trends can be short lived, and when the market recovers, cheap "value" stocks often bounce back.

As we observed in an earlier chapter, some of the stocks that underperform today may spring back tomorrow. As Horace said, *"Many shall be restored that now are fallen and many shall fall that now are in honor."*⁷

THE ETF INVESTOR

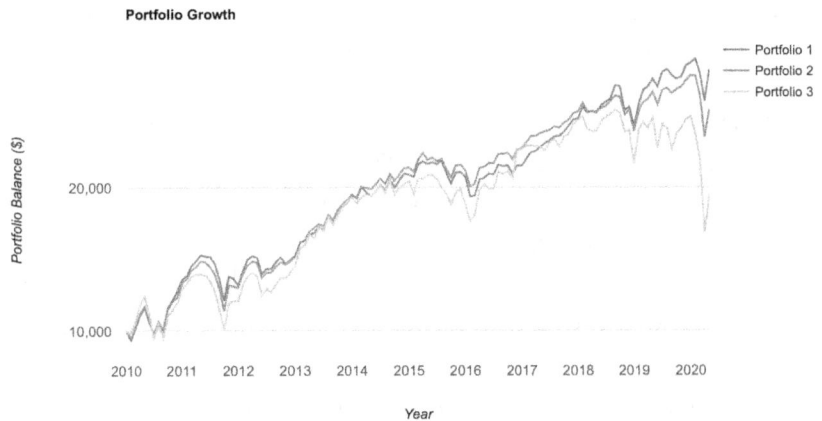

Three mid-cap ETFs. Data from March 31, 2020. Source: Portfolio Visualizer

Portfolio | Initial Balance | Final Balance | CAGR

- Portfolio 1 - IMCG $10,000 $35,122 12.93%
- Portfolio 2 - VO $10,000 $29,001 10.85%
- Portfolio 3 - RFV $10,000 $19,248 6.54%

As much as I may be tempted to steer clear of RFV because it has fallen mightily, I'm not counting it out. That fund may be out of favor today but one day they may be restored.

One quality I've noticed in all good investors is the ability to be patient and just observe what's happening around them. Regardless of whether you're interested in mid-cap ETFs, I think it makes sense to be aware of ETFs like these so you can track the returns of these niche asset classes over time.

I find it instructive to revisit these three ETFs in upcoming years to see if IMCG continues its outperformance, or if an ETF like RFV bounces back. The process observing ETF performance in different investing cycles can help you see that asset classes do not all move together, and sometimes having mid-caps, or value stocks in your ETFs can provide better long-term returns than only owning large-caps.

Update one year later — May 27, 2021.

As part of the 2021 update to this book, it is worth noting that the one-year performance of RFV (value **91.36%**) has greatly outpaced VO (blend, **45.73%**) and IMCG (growth, **42.55%**).[8]

This is a useful piece of data because it shows that even though the growth style was popular for a long time, from the period between 2020-2021 (and perhaps this will continue for some time), *mid-cap value stocks more than doubled* the returns of mid-cap growth stocks.

This observation is especially piercing because it shows how those stocks that had low valuations before and during the pandemic suddenly snapped back into favor when some light appeared at the end of the tunnel. The value recovery began in the fall of 2020 when a vaccine and return to post-pandemic life became a possibility, and the prices of stocks of companies poised to benefit shot up powerfully.

Mid-cap ETF Summary

Mid-caps tend to exhibit performance somewhere in between the wild swings and fast growth of small caps and the solidity of many of the large caps. Mid cap fluctuations are not always quite as wide as those you might observe in small caps.

A mid cap ETF makes sense for investors who own large or small cap funds and would like exposure to a new asset class. Additionally, they might find mid-cap ETFs to be excellent as stand-alone investments because they combine qualities of both small and large cap companies.

15

VANECK VECTORS MORNINGSTAR WIDE MOAT

VanEck Vectors Morningstar Wide Moat ETF (MOAT)

The stocks in this ETF have "wide moats," which is another way of saying they have *durable competitive advantages* that help companies resist competition. The financial services company Morningstar has a filter which selects stocks of wide-moats companies, and this ETF invests according to that list.

This actively managed ETF is different from the diversified "core" portfolios of hundreds or thousands of stocks discussed earlier; it holds only 47 stocks[1]. This ETF's concentration gives it a chance to deliver performance in excess of diversified funds because of this concentration in a small number of stocks and its focus on wide moat companies. It could also do worse if its stocks underperform.

Many ETFs are so broadly diversified that their holdings mirror the S&P 500. They *claim* to be actively managed, but in practice they are just "hugging" the index, buying essentially the same stocks as the index fund. They own so many stocks — often 300 to 500 stocks — that they can't beat the market *because they are the market.* You may want to avoid paying a steep expense ratio for an ETF that's a copy of an index ETF you can own at low cost.

MOAT does not hug an index: with fewer than 50 stocks and a focus on wide moat companies that resist competition, this ETF has a chance to provide returns that diverge from those of the S&P 500. Again, there's no way of saying it will achieve this goal, but for those who want to try, this fund could provide a way to attempt to beat the index.

MOAT has performed well over the past 3- and 5-year periods, generating returns of 7.48% and 9.39%[2] respectively, compared to Vanguard S&P 500 ETF (VOO) which has generated returns of 6.16% and 7.22% during these periods.

VanEck Vectors Morningstar Wide Moat ETF (MOAT)

Top 15 Holdings[3]
Expense ratio: .48%
Symbol/Holding/ % Assets

1. GILD Gilead Sciences Inc 3.28%
2. AMZN Amazon.com Inc 3.15%
3. VEEV Veeva Systems Inc 3.13%
4. BIIB Biogen Inc 3.04%
5. INTC Intel Corp 2.96%
6. K Kellogg Co 2.91%
7. PFE Pfizer Inc 2.90%
8. CAT Caterpillar Inc 2.87%
9. BLK BlackRock Inc 2.75%
10. PM Philip Morris International Inc 2.71%
11. NOW ServiceNow Inc 2.69%
12. MRK Merck & Co Inc 2.69%
13. NKE Nike Inc 2.60%
14. BRK.B Berkshire Hathaway Inc 2.56%
15. CTVA Corteva Inc 2.56%

The top holdings are dominant companies in their sectors. These companies have wide moats that provide durable competitive advantages which help protect these businesses from competitors' attempts to take their customers.

MOAT may be a strong addition to a portfolio that already has a diversified ETF like VOO, VTI or VT, or one could hold it as a stand-alone fund.

16

O'SHARES GLOBAL INTERNET GIANTS

O'Shares Global Internet Giants ETF (OGIG)

O'Shares Global Internet Giants ETF (OGIG) is a rules-based ETF designed to provide investors with the means to invest in some of the largest global companies that derive most of their revenue from the Internet and e-commerce sectors that exhibit quality and growth potential[1].

This ETF is less than two years old at the time of this writing, and as a result, it does not have much performance history. Its stock holdings have performed extremely well since inception, and this ETF, while still small in terms of total assets under management compared to other tech funds, has performed well.

OGIG owns a blend of SaaS stocks (software as a service) as well as other technology stocks. These groups have done very well during the past several years as companies that do business on line have greatly outperformed traditional "brick-and-mortar" businesses.

This online presence has provided an even greater edge during the pandemic because people do most of their purchases online and also spend more time using searching the Internet and less time in physical stores.

O'Shares Global Internet Giants ETF (OGIG)

Top 15 Holdings[2]
Expense ratio: .48%
Symbol/ Holding / % Assets

1. AMZN Amazon.com Inc 6.23%
2. GOOGL Alphabet Inc 5.53%
3. MSFT Microsoft Corp 5.28%
4. 700 Tencent Holdings Ltd 4.92%
5. BABA Alibaba Group Holding Ltd 4.79%
6. FB Facebook Inc 4.53%
7. W Wayfair Inc 2.85%
8. SHOP Shopify Inc 2.50%
9. PDD Pinduoduo Inc 2.09%
10. CRWD Crowdstrike Holdings Inc 2.03%
11. NFLX Netflix Inc 1.85%
12. ZM Zoom Video Communications Inc 1.82%
13. 3690 Meituan Dianping 1.81%
14. SNAP Snap Inc 1.78%
15. NOW ServiceNow Inc 1.69%

Number of Holdings: 71
Percent Assets in Top 15: 49.66%

As this book goes to press OGIG has pulled off quite a 2020. In the year of Coronavirus, those who own these shares have done well. The fund's +21.12% return as of May 14th, 2020 put it in the top 1% of its technology category and well ahead of the -12.40% return of the S&P 500 index[3].

This is a relatively new ETF that started on Jun 05, 2018. Since the ETF is not even two years old it is too early to say if its strategy will continue to outperform.

This sector fund will most likely perform well when technology and Internet stocks shine, but I would only think of it as a niche ETF to supplement a diversified portfolio.

My only problem with this ETF has nothing to do with the quality of companies selected, but rather that the top three are top holdings of the S&P 500, and the four and five spots (Tencent and Alibaba) are two large emerging-market companies.

An investor could gain exposure to these stocks by investing in ETFs with rock-bottom expenses like VOO (.03% expense ratio) and VWO (.10% expense ratio). Those two ETFs let you own Amazon, Google, Microsoft, Tencent, and Alibaba for while paying very little in annual expenses. OGIG charges you seven times as much (.48% expense ratio) for the convenience of owning an ETF marketed as an Internet fund.

Having all of these names in one fund provides convenience, and I suppose each investor has to decide how much they want to pay. Because most brokerage firms offer commission-free trades, it would seem to be a better decision to just buy shares of a few large cap tech stocks or ETFs that hold them instead of paying .48% in yearly expenses to own them in an actively-managed ETF.

I've taken a closer look at several "Internet" ETFs and I notice that many of them rely heavily on large cap tech stocks: First Trust Dow Jones Internet (FDN) charges .62% and its top holdings include Amazon, Facebook, Adobe and Alphabet.

Similarly, Invesco NASDAQ Internet (PNQI) lists Amazon, Facebook, Adobe and Alphabet as top holdings and *also* charges an expense ratio of .62%. *Are you seeing a trend here?* These ETF providers are just packaging stocks you could own dirt-cheap in a large cap fund (or buy commission-free) and charging you a high expense ratio.

I do like the mixture of Internet stocks in OGIG, but I believe investors should take a look under the hood and decide for themselves if it's worth the convenience to pay for stocks they could own cheaply in another ETF.

ARK Next Generation Internet ETF (ARKW) provides divergence from the typical large-cap tech stock names. It's a volatile fund, and I don't think it makes sense for anyone except those with strong stomachs. ARKW does not sell you the same four large tech stocks. This fund owns a mixture of Internet stocks that you might not have heard of or bought on your own, and if you're going to pay for active management it makes sense to invest in a fund that buys stocks that diverge from the usual large-cap tech fare.

ARKW's top holding is Tesla at 10%,[4] and this large commitment to Tesla is typical of Ark Funds: of the five ETFs Ark manages, three of them list Tesla as the #1 holding. I admire the Ark funds' boldness, but I am wary of ETFs that charge .75% and then invest 10% of the fund in a stock like Tesla you could buy commission-fee without recurring annual expense.

Even with my reservations about paying high fees to own an ETF that's overweighted in large tech stocks, I like OGIG (as well as ARKW) because they both possess a unique blend of innovative companies leading the way in the Internet age.

Taking a step back, I think it is worth seeing the forest for the trees, and if investors have to pay .48% or .75%, yet their investment beats the market by 10% a year, then clearly it's a good investment. While I don't own an Internet ETF, I will keep my eye on them because I want to know if any of these ETFs possess an edge when it comes to crushing it in the Internet sector. It's like 1999 all over again...

17

ARK INNOVATION

ARK Innovation (ARKK)

ARK Innovation invests according to ARK's investment theme of "disruptive innovation," which it defines as buying stocks of technologies that potentially change the way the world works[1]. This ETF is an actively managed fund that a rational investor would only buy as an "add on" investment to an already diversified ETF strategy.

This ETF, run by fund-manager-du-jour Cathy Woods, is the flagship fund for a company that has truly crushed it with ETFs. There is no denying that she has the Midas touch when it comes to picking stocks: the only question is whether her success in beating the market will endure, or if we're witnessing someone with a hot hand at the stock casino.

ARK Invest, which manages ARK Innovation, explains their mission this way: "We Invest Solely In Disruptive Innovation." They accomplish this by investing in companies that develop products or services related to technology and scientific research. They focus their investments in DNA technologies, energy, automation, and financial services technologies.[2]

ARK Innovation (ARKK)

Top 15 Holdings
  Expense ratio: .75%
  Symbol/Holding/% Assets

  1. TSLA Tesla Inc 10.51%
  2. ILMN Illumina Inc 8.26%
  3. NVTA Invitae Corp 7.06%
  4. SQ Square Inc 6.57%
  5. SSYS Stratasys Ltd 4.96%
  6. CRSP CRISPR Therapeutics AG 4.89%
  7. ROKU Roku Inc 4.56%
  8. TWOU 2U Inc 4.04%
  9. NTLA Intellia Therapeutics Inc 3.98%
  10. PRLB Proto Labs Inc 3.88%
  11. XLNX Xilinx Inc 3.50%
  12. EDIT Editas Medicine Inc 3.23%
  13. Z Zillow Group Inc 3.15%
  14. NSTG NanoString Technologies Inc 2.82%
  15. MTLS Materialise NV 2.42%

Number of Holdings: 33
Percent Assets in Top 10: 74.21%

This ETF has a higher expense ratio than most other funds featured in this book, but keep in mind this is no passively managed index. In most cases, you will find that actively managed ETFs come with a higher price than the fund's passively managed cousins.

With most things in life, you get what you pay for. With investing, it's often the other way around: you get what you *don't* pay for, meaning you get to keep all the investment returns that you don't pay for in fees.

However, passively managed index funds might not always

provide you with the unique combination of stocks you want to own. ARKK may be one of the cases where you are willing to pay more than the passively managed index for a fund whose investment managers may have expertise that leads to market-beating returns. If you pay .75% in management fees and you consistently beat the market by 10% then you're doing pretty good.

This fund might be just the ticket for an investor who likes a heavy chunk of Telsa along with genomics stocks like gene sequencing titan Illumina, genetic testing company Invitae, and payment processor Square.

This highly concentrated ETF portfolio holds only 37 stocks, with 71.25% of them in the top 15 holdings[3]. The three largest "elements" of the portfolio are 3D printing, gene therapy, and e-commerce[4].

This ETF may be a useful option for investors who already have a core ETF with more broad-based exposure and would like to allocate some of their investment toward fast-growing, tech-dominated companies.

ARKK is a concentrated fund, a "high octane" ETF that swings for the fences, and investors who want to invest in companies involved in bold innovation may want to take a close look at this fund.

18

WISDOMTREE CLOUD COMPUTING

WisdomTree Cloud Computing (WCLD)

This ETF invests in companies involved in cloud computing and provides exposure to emerging, fast-growing U.S.-listed companies that are focused on cloud software and services.

WCLD tracks the Nasdaq Emerging Cloud Index, an equally weighted index designed to measure the performance of emerging cloud-based software companies.[1]

This is a relatively new ETF with an inception date of September 4, 2019, so it got up and running just before the pandemic hit. This fund's first full year has coincided with the most volatile stock market in recent history, and its portfolio has endured this baptism by fire and emerged with flying colors.

As of this writing, the fund is in the top 1% of its category and has delivered YTD returns of 35.85% while the S&P 500, for the sake of comparison, has returned -5.04%[2]. This is significant outperformance when viewed against all of the other companies. One thing that stands out about this portfolio is that the component companies are in a variety of different sectors. This spreads risk out among different areas of the economy.

Because WCLD focuses on companies that conduct some or all of their business using cloud computing, this fund's holdings have benefited as people work from home and depend on the remote delivery of services that cloud computing provides.

These three factors make WCLD stand out from many ETFs in this book. I especially admire these three factors:

- Unlike some of the Internet ETFs mentioned in a previous chapter, this fund does not load its top spots with the big four tech companies. I like this because you can own those stocks at a low cost through a passively managed index fund.
- The top holding — Zoom Video Communications — only comprises 2.79% of the portfolio[3]. Though this percent will change with Zoom's stock price, I think it's worth noting that this fund has performed extremely well with a *relatively small allocation to Zoom*, which has been a superstar stock during the pandemic. I like that this ETF does not rely too heavily on just one stock. This tells me that *many of the stocks are pulling their weight in the portfolio.* It's easy for a fund to have 10% in a few tech high-flyers and do well. But why pay a fee for an ETF heavy on a stock you could buy with no commission and no annual expense ratio?
- WCLD is a solid example of an actively managed fund that buys a variety of stocks I may never have discovered on my own, and I appreciate that the portfolio invests in a niche comprised of 53 cloud computing stocks.

WisdomTree Cloud Computing (WCLD)

Top 15 Holdings[4]
    Expense ratio: .45%
    Symbol/ Holding / % Assets

1. ZM Zoom Video Communications Inc 2.79%
2. FIVN Five9 Inc 2.75%
3. SHOP Shopify Inc 2.68%
4. ZS Zscaler Inc 2.54%
5. EVBG Everbridge Inc 2.53%
6. DOCU DocuSign Inc 2.48%
7. OKTA Okta Inc 2.36%
8. VEEV Veeva Systems Inc 2.30%
9. CRWD Crowdstrike Holdings Inc 2.27%
10. TEAM Atlassian Corporation PLC 2.27%
11. NET Cloudflare Inc 2.26%
12. COUP Coupa Software Inc 2.22%
13. QLYS Qualys Inc 2.20%
14. SMAR Smartsheet Inc 2.14%
15. TWOU 2U Inc 2.14%

Number of Holdings: 53
Percent Assets in Top 15: 35.94%

This ETF invests in a narrow slice of technology stocks — the subset of software companies that provide cloud-based software services. This fund is a way to invest in software companies distinct from the well-known mega-tech software names like Adobe, Alphabet, Microsoft, or Salesforce. These small software companies may grow faster than larger, established companies they are starting from a smaller base.

Many of these companies only sell one product or service, so they're much riskier as well, because if demand for one company's product or service slows or stops, or if a competitor starts taking customers, they may not have other revenue streams to fall back on. Some of these fast-growing stocks can go out of business if things don't go their way, so if you want to invest in them it's probably better to own a variety of risky bets as part of a larger portfolio.

By owning many risky stocks, an ETF like this one protects

investors from any one company's failure from having an impact on the fund, because with 53 stocks, most stocks makes up on average less than 2% of the fund. This ETF could be useful to an investor who already owns some larger "core" or large tech ETFs and would like to gain exposure to smaller, fast-growing cloud computing companies.

19

SPDR S&P BIOTECH

SPDR S&P Biotech ETF (XBI)

As this book goes to press many biotech companies are scurrying to develop a vaccine for Coronavirus. Other companies are trying to develop quick and accurate testing. Still, others are trying to develop a drug or combination of drugs to cure patients.

Wouldn't it be great if you could identify the winning companies? *If only it were that easy.* The truth is that hundreds of biotech companies are working around the clock trying to find solutions, and no one knows which companies will be successful. We will only know the winners in hindsight.

You would gamble trying to bet on AstraZeneca, BioNTech, Novovax, Inovio, Johnson & Johnson, Moderna or PfizerModerna will be the best vaccine stocks, but it's hard to know which one (or ones) will be most successful.

There's a solution to this problem of risking it all on one spin of the wheel. You can get a biotech ETF. That way you extract all of the juicy goodness from the biotech sector without fear of picking the stock that goes nowhere and loses 30% of its value in one day. This

ETF and the one featured on the next page provide exposure to the entire biotech sector with reduced company-specific risk.

SPDR S&P Biotech (XBI)

Top 15 Holdings[1]
Expense ratio: .35%
Symbol/ Holding / % Assets

1. MRNA Moderna Inc 3.48%
2. EXEL Exelixis Inc 2.52%
3. REGN Regeneron Pharmaceuticals Inc 2.51%
4. SGEN Seattle Genetics Inc 2.47%
5. IMMU Immunomedics Inc 2.38%
6. UTHR United Therapeutics Corp 2.16%
7. VRTX Vertex Pharmaceuticals Inc 2.12%
8. ALNY Alnylam Pharmaceuticals Inc 2.11%
9. BMRN Biomarin Pharmaceutical Inc 2.03%
10. GILD Gilead Sciences Inc 2.02%
11. ACAD ACADIA Pharmaceuticals Inc 1.86%
12. GBT Global Blood Therapeutics Inc 1.82%
13. INCY Incyte Corp 1.80%
14. BIIB Biogen Inc 1.77%
15. AMGN Amgen Inc 1.71%

Number of Holdings: 122
Percentage of Assets in Top 15: 32.74%

20

ISHARES NASDAQ BIOTECHNOLOGY

iShares Nasdaq Biotechnology ETF (IBB)

Top 15 Holdings[1]
   Expense ratio: .47%
   Symbol / Holding / % Assets

1. AMGN Amgen Inc 8.50%
2. GILD Gilead Sciences Inc 8.03%
3. VRTX Vertex Pharmaceuticals Inc 7.97%
4. REGN Regeneron Pharmaceuticals Inc 6.81%
5. BIIB Biogen Inc 6.08%
6. ILMN Illumina Inc 4.27%
7. SGEN Seattle Genetics Inc 3.28%
8. ALXN Alexion Pharmaceuticals Inc 2.48%
9. INCY Incyte Corp 2.41%
10. MRNA Moderna Inc 2.09%
11. BMRN Biomarin Pharmaceutical Inc 1.98%
12. ALNY Alnylam Pharmaceuticals Inc 1.89%
13. SNY Sanofi SA 1.19%

14. TECH Bio-Techne Corp 1.16%
15. NBIX Neurocrine Biosciences Inc 1.10%

Number of Holdings: 210
Percentage of Assets in Top 15: 59.23%

I think it will be worth comparing XBI with IBB so you can see how they compare to one another. This can help you see differences.

Comparison of XBI (top) and IBB, two biotech ETFs. Source: Portfolio Visualizer - website: portfoliovisualizer.com

As you can see from the graph above, the two ETFs experienced similar performance until 2016 when returns for XBI began to outpace those of IBB.

Portfolio | Initial Balance | Final Balance | CAGR[2]

- Portfolio 1 - XBI $10,000 $52,799 13.38%
- Portfolio 2 - IBB $10,000 $42,650 11.57%

In the period between 2007 and 2020 XBI (.35% expense ratio) outperformed IBB (.47% expense ratio) by almost 2%.

All things being equal I prefer to invest in ETFs with lower expenses, and in this case, XBI has a lower expense ratio of the two funds. Keep in mind that past performance does not predict future returns, and it's impossible to predict which fund will outperform in the future.

21

VANGUARD HEALTH CARE

Vanguard Health Care (VHT)

I think it's worth taking a look at this ETF because it invests in stocks that investors might like if they want to invest in some of the fast-growing biotech and also in more traditional healthcare and pharmaceutical stocks.

This is an extremely low-cost ETF, charging only .10%, which means that you would pay only $10 a year to invest $10,000.

Vanguard Health Care ETF (VHT)

Top 15 Holdings[1]
   Expense ratio: .10%
   Symbol/ Holding / % Assets

   1. JNJ Johnson & Johnson 8.96%
   2. UNH UnitedHealth Group Inc 6.29%
   3. PFE Pfizer Inc 4.90%
   4. MRK Merck & Co Inc 4.51%
   5. ABT Abbott Laboratories 3.70%
   6. BMY Bristol-Myers Squibb Co 3.29%

7. AMGN Amgen Inc 3.23%
8. LLY Eli Lilly and Co 3.11%
9. TMO Thermo Fisher Scientific Inc 3.09%
10. MDT Medtronic PLC 2.98%
11. ABBV Abbvie Inc 2.90%
12. DHR Danaher Corp 2.36%
13. GILD Gilead Sciences Inc 2.25%
14. CVS CVS Health Corp 1.81%
15. BDX Becton Dickinson and Co 1.61%

Number of Holdings: 382
Percent Assets in Top 15: 55.00%

You can see that Amgen and Gilead Sciences are among the top 15 holdings of the biotech ETFs discussed earlier, but VHT invests in *both of those biotech companies* and *also invests in a variety of other larger and well-established health care companies* like Johnson & Johnson, Pfizer, and Merck.

VHT is a solid choice for investors who want to own health care and pharmaceutical stocks with a small amount of exposure to biotech, but not as much as you'd find in the focused biotech ETFs discussed in previous chapters.

22

THREE DIVIDEND ETFS

What's in a name? Well, there's a lot in a name to mislead you if rely only on the name when comparing ETFs.

Let's say you decide to buy an ETF that invests in dividend-paying stocks. There are lots of funds that say, "I'm a dividend fund," and they've got the word "dividend" in their name. Yet the criteria they use to select dividend-paying stocks can be wildly different.

You must look beyond the ETF name to see which stocks the fund owns, which you can do by searching for the fund's ticker symbol and the word "holdings." You want to see the specific stocks the fund owns and make sure it invests in solid companies.

You want to make sure you understand what kind of stocks the ETF owns and the list of holdings and the ETFs annual report are both good sources of information. Keep in mind that ETF names can be misleading and you can wind up owning a bunch of junky stocks.

For example, there has been a lot of interest in dividend-paying stocks lately, and as a result, people looking to buy dividend ETFs might do a quick search and invest in one of them without looking carefully at what they're buying.

I will show you three extremely different ETFs that all have the

THE ETF INVESTOR

word "dividend" in the title. You need to know a couple of things about dividends for this to make sense.

1. Dividends are cash payments that a company pays investors. These payments are usually made every quarter, and sometimes monthly.
2. The amount of the dividend is expressed as the dividend yield, which is calculated by dividing the annual dividend amount by the stock price[1]. For example, if a company's annual dividend is $1.50 and the stock trades at $25, the dividend yield is 6% ($1.50 ÷ $25).

At the time of this writing, a 6% dividend is currently considered an extremely high payout, and *many investors would be delighted* with it. But what happens when there are problems with a company and it has fallen out of favor? For example, many oil, banking, and real estate investment trust (REIT) stocks are getting hammered during the Coronavirus pandemic.

Using the example above, if the dividend is $1.50 and suddenly the stock price drops from $25 to $12.50, the dividend yield is now 12% ($1.50 ÷ $12.50). That 12% dividend is now incredibly high, but the problem is the stock price has halved because the company is in trouble.

A dividend ETF may hold companies that go out of business, or they may stop paying or reduce their dividend payouts. The ETF you own will get clobbered if too many of its holdings are junky companies.

Three Dividend ETFs

Let's take a closer look under the hood of three ETFs with the word *dividend* in the title: Blackrock iShares Core Dividend Growth (DGRO), ProShares S&P 500 (Dividend) Aristocrats fund (NOBL), and Global X Super dividend fund (SDIV).[2]

23

BLACKROCK ISHARES CORE DIVIDEND GROWTH

Blackrock iShares Core Dividend Growth (DGRO)
SEC 30-Day Yield 2.70%[1]

iShares Core Dividend Growth is one ETF with the word "dividend" in the title. It invests in companies that have a history of sustained dividend growth, and its holdings are diversified across many industries[2]. It owns the big companies we know well — Microsoft, Johnson & Johnson, Apple, Chevron, Verizon, JP Morgan Chase, etc. *These are among the largest, most consistent dividend-paying companies in the US.*

Blackrock iShares Core Dividend Growth (DGRO)

Top 15 Holdings[3]
   Expense ratio: .08%
   Symbol/ Holding / % Assets

   1. MSFT Microsoft Corp 3.53%
   2. AAPL Apple Inc 3.19%
   3. JNJ Johnson & Johnson 3.17%

4. CVX Chevron Corp 2.99%
5. VZ Verizon Communications Inc 2.91%
6. PFE Pfizer Inc 2.84%
7. JPM JPMorgan Chase & Co 2.72%
8. PG Procter & Gamble Co 2.13%
9. CSCO Cisco Systems Inc 1.86%
10. INTC Intel Corp 1.86%
11. HD Home Depot Inc 1.76%
12. WFC Wells Fargo & Co 1.76%
13. MRK Merck & Co Inc 1.71%
14. BAC Bank of America Corp 1.62%
15. AVGO Broadcom Inc 1.56%

Number of Holdings: 479
Percent Assets in Top 15: 35.62%

24

PROSHARES S&P 500 DIVIDEND ARISTOCRATS FUND

ProShares S&P 500 (Dividend) Aristocrats fund (NOBL)
 SEC 30-Day Yield 2.47%[1]

I'd like to share a few details about this ETF you might not see at first glance. First, this fund *does not prioritize giving you the highest dividend yield*. Instead, this fund *aims to invest in quality companies* and buys stocks that have been paying dividends for at least 25 years, with most doing so for 40 years or more[2].

As a side note, the expense ratio is 4x higher than the iShares Core Dividend Growth. That's not necessarily bad, but it's worth noting that you're giving up some return that you could otherwise keep and paying it to the ETF provider.

Let's take a look at the holdings, and keep in mind that this ETF prioritizes consistency of dividend payment.

ProShares S&P 500 (Dividend) Aristocrats fund (NOBL)

Top 15 Holdings[3]
 Expense ratio: .35%

THE ETF INVESTOR

Symbol/ Holding / % Assets

1. LOW Lowe's Companies Inc 1.73%
2. ROP Roper Technologies Inc 1.68%
3. BEN Franklin Resources Inc 1.68%
4. ECL Ecolab Inc 1.65%
5. AOS A. O. Smith Corp 1.65%
6. PNR Pentair PLC 1.64%
7. TGT Target Corp 1.64%
8. TROW T. Rowe Price Group Inc 1.64%
9. GWW WW Grainger Inc 1.63%
10. ROST Ross Stores Inc 1.61%
11. NUE Nucor Corp 1.61%
12. BF.B Brown-Forman Corp 1.60%
13. ADP Automatic Data Processing Inc 1.60%
14. O Realty Income Corp 1.60%
15. APD Air Products and Chemicals Inc 1.59%

Number of Holdings: 67
Percent Assets in Top 15: 24.54%

25

GLOBAL X SUPER DIVIDEND FUND

Global X Super Dividend Fund (SDIV)
30-Day SEC Yield 14.28%[1]

Global X Super Dividend Fund takes a different approach to dividend investing compared to the "Dividend Aristocrat" fund outlined in the prior chapter. SDIV scans the database of all stocks and mechanically *buys only the highest dividend-paying stocks in the world.*

So, what happens is that you wind up with stocks whose prices may be very low compared to their dividends. This is not always a good situation, because their stock prices may be low because of problems with the company or sector.

An investor in this ETF needs to be aware of this strategy, because you could wind up with a pretty *junky portfolio of high dividend stocks* because the stock price (the denominator of the dividend yield equation discussed earlier) is plunging. In the short term, an investor might collect a high dividend, but in the long term, the value of the stocks in this ETFs could decline rapidly. That could severely impair an investor's returns.

I heard an episode of The Rational Reminder podcast[2] featuring

THE ETF INVESTOR

ETF expert David Nadig. During the discussion, Nadig pointed out that even though SDIV has the word "dividend" in the title, it is an entirely different portfolio than NOBL. "[They are] *Radically* different portfolios. *Crazily* different portfolios," he said.

Nadig said NOBL "looks like an old-school, widows-and-orphans blue chip ETF," yet both NOBL and SDIV show up on the same lists of dividend ETFs because they attract a lot of money, and they both have the word *dividend* in their names.

Global X Super Dividend Fund (SDIV)

Top 15 Holdings[3]
  Expense ratio: .58%
  Symbol/ Holding / % Assets

  1. DGOC Diversified Gas & Oil PLC 2.22%
  2. BGS B&G Foods Inc 2.00%
  3. JAS-R Jasmine International PCL 1.63%
  4. KIO Kumba Iron Ore Ltd 1.58%
  5. BAT British American Tobacco (Malaysia) Bhd 1.57%
  6. PNL PostNL NV 1.54%
  7. 338 Sinopec Shanghai Petrochemical Co Ltd 1.53%
  8. NHC New Hope Corporation Ltd 1.51%
  9. RMG Royal Mail PLC 1.50%
  10. ALTR Altri SGPS SA 1.45%
  11. SVST Severstal' PAO 1.44%
  12. IMB Imperial Brands PLC 1.43%
  13. 1908 C&D International Investment Group Ltd 1.42%
  14. ZENITHBANK Zenith Bank PLC 1.42%
  15. VGR Vector Group Ltd 1.41%

  Number of Holdings: 101
  Percent Assets in Top 15: 23.65%

. . .

How do you avoid buying into a dividend fund that might not be what you expect? You have to look at the holdings, and as Nadig said, "The narrower and the weirder the thing you're chasing, the more you have to look under the hood."

When you look under the hood you will see that SDIV scans the database of all stocks and mechanically buys the highest dividend stocks. So, you end up with pretty junky stocks because the stock price (the denominator of the dividend yield equation) is falling, which drives the yield higher. Dividend investors who don't check ETF holdings might be drawn to high yields like moths to a flame.

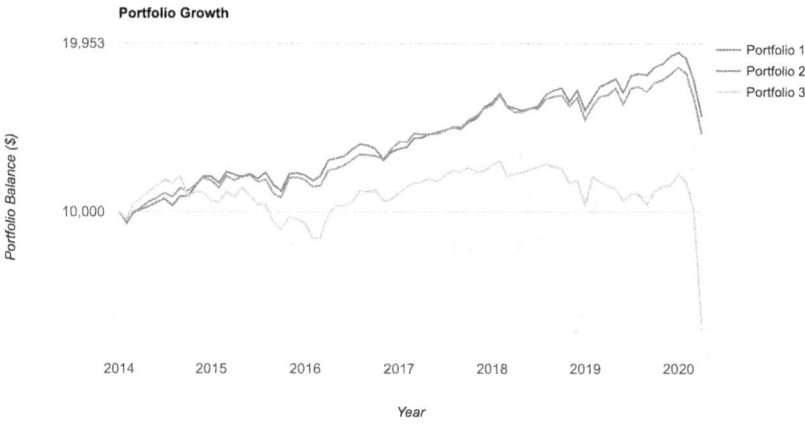

This graph compares DGRO (top), NOBL(middle), and SDIV (bottom). DGRO select stocks based a history of sustained dividend growth, NOBL focuses on consistent dividend payouts over 25 to 40 years, and SDIV mechanically selects the highest dividend payers. Image Source: Portfolio Visualizer based on returns as of April 8, 2020.

Portfolio | Initial Balance | Final Balance | CAGR

- Portfolio 1 - DGRO $10,000 $14,778 6.45%
- Portfolio 2 - NOBL $10,000 $13,766 5.25%
- Portfolio 3 - SDIV $10,000 $6,172 -7.43%

SDIV may attract investors drawn to the high dividend, but the shortcut of picking dividend ETFs judging by those with the highest yield is flawed because the stock price in the dividend yield equation may be falling because there are serious problems with the company.

Think about whether stocks in the ETF will pay out 14% in dividends year after year; you'll agree that it's pretty unlikely. Also, you'll notice that many of these companies might cut their dividends or go out of business. Protect yourself by looking beyond the word "dividend" in the ETF name to make sure you are aware of the quality of the companies in the ETF's holdings before you invest.

26

ARK FINTECH INNOVATION

Ark Fintech Innovation (ARKF)

This ETF provides investors with a focused way to invest in the financial technology, or "fintech" sector. These companies employ newly developed digital and online technologies in the banking and financial services industries[1].

ARKF owns several stocks I've often thought of buying, but I never bought them because I always wanted to do a little more "due diligence" before investing. I do a lot of research before buying any individual stock, and the fast-growing fintech sector was always a bit too fast moving for me to gain any serious understanding. I have first-hand experience with Square because I use it often in my business, but after that I don't have much background in digital payments and financial technology.

This is an actively managed ETF, and that sets it apart from many of the passively managed index ETFs we've discussed earlier in this book. ARKF aims to grow investor money by investing in domestic and foreign fintech stocks that include these platforms[2]:

- Transaction Innovations
- Blockchain Technology

- Risk Transformation
- Frictionless Funding Platforms
- Customer Facing Platforms
- New Intermediaries

This ETF invests in a wide range of companies, from small caps like Lending Tree and Pinterest to large caps like Alibaba, Apple, Amazon, PayPal, and Tencent.

ARKF provides wide geographic distribution as well, including companies outside the United States: Adyen (Netherlands), Z Holdings (Japan), Mercadolibre (Argentina), and several companies in Hong Kong, China, and Taiwan[3].

While there are many countries represented in the portfolio, I was surprised at the omission of two fast-growing Brazilian payment processors: The Stone Company and Pagamentos Seguros, both prime exemplars of the fast-growing fintech sector. When I saw the wide range of countries represented in this fund I was surprised not to see the two Brazilian companies.

Ark Fintech Innovation is an exciting portfolio that warrants a closer look from an investor who already has a diversified portfolio of core investments and wants to focus on this fast-growing sector.

Ark Fintech Innovation (ARKF)

Top 15 Holdings[4]
Expense ratio: .75%
Symbol/ Holding / % Assets

1. SQ Square Inc 11.65%
2. MELI Mercadolibre Inc 5.76%
3. AAPL Apple Inc 4.68%
4. Z Zillow Group Inc 4.66%
5. TCEHY Tencent Holdings Ltd 4.57%
6. TREE LendingTree Inc 3.96%
7. PYPL PayPal Holdings Inc 3.82%

8. 3690 Meituan Dianping 3.80%
9. PDD Pinduoduo Inc 3.64%
10. BABA Alibaba Group Holding Ltd 3.39%
11. PINS Pinterest Inc 3.38%
12. AMZN Amazon.com Inc 3.13%
13. 4689 Z Holdings Corp 2.99%
14. ADYEN Adyen NV 2.88%
15. SPLK Splunk Inc 2.81%

I'd like to share a few thoughts about this ETF's expense ratio. Just like its cousin, Ark Innovation, which we looked at in Chapter 14, Ark Fintech Innovation charges a .75% expense ratio. Now, my view on ETF expenses is that you want to keep them as low as possible — any fees you pay are the market's return that goes into the fund company's pocket and not into yours. However, I have no problem paying higher expenses if it means I'll have a chance to own new stocks that these active managers pick — stocks I might not come across on my own.

One thing that I notice is that this ARKF is that it owns stocks of large companies like Apple ($1.47 trillion), Amazon ($1.27 trillion), Alibaba ($583.9 billion), and PayPal ($182.27 billion) that you can own in an S&P 500 fund with a rock-bottom expense ratio of .05% or less. I don't like having to pay 15 times as much to own those stocks in an ETF.

I would prefer a focused ETF like ARKF to own stocks that investors might not find in an S&P 500 fund that they can own at a low cost. The benefit of a fund like ARKF is to find companies that I might not find by myself or own in some other large-cap fund.

ARKF is a relatively new fund, and the 1-year return of 33.27% places it in the top 19% of funds in the Morningstar US Technology category as of Jun 12, 2020. Perhaps its best relative performance is its 22.16% YTD return compared to the S&P 500 index' -5.04% YTD[5].

As you can see, this fund has outperformed the S&P 500 by more than 27% during an extremely volatile year. In my opinion, one of the reasons for the wild outperformance is the absence of airlines, cruise lines, hotels, oil companies, and real estate or vacation-related stocks in the portfolio.

The fintech sector dodged a major bullet during the pandemic, and this new fund shows the benefits of an actively managed sector ETF that mainly focuses on stocks in a narrow sector — like fintech — that often get diluted by or omitted from large-cap portfolios.

ARKF is an attractive offering for investors who already have a diversified core portfolio and are looking for a focused way to invest in this stock market niche.

27

TECHNOLOGY SECTOR ETFS

There are many tech sector ETFs available, but I think we can get a good handle on what most of them look like by examining these three funds.

Invesco QQQ Trust (QQQ)

Top 15 Holdings[1]
    Expense ratio: .20%
    Symbol/ Holding / % Assets

1. MSFT Microsoft Corp 11.83%
2. AAPL Apple Inc 11.42%
3. AMZN Amazon.com Inc 9.97%
4. FB Facebook Inc 4.30%
5. GOOGL Alphabet Inc 4.01%
6. GOOG Alphabet Inc 3.99%
7. INTC Intel Corp 2.74%
8. NVDA NVIDIA Corp 2.05%
9. NFLX Netflix Inc 2.05%

THE ETF INVESTOR

10. PEP PepsiCo Inc 2.00%
11. CSCO Cisco Systems Inc 1.96%
12. ADBE Adobe Inc 1.91%
13. PYPL PayPal Holdings Inc 1.83%
14. CMCSA Comcast Corp 1.78%
15. TSLA Tesla Inc 1.62%

Number of Holdings: 104
Percent Assets in Top 15: 63.47%

Vanguard Information Technology Index Fund ETF Shares (VGT)

Top 15 Holdings[2]
Expense ratio: .10%
Symbol/ Holding / % Assets

1. AAPL Apple Inc 18.90%
2. MSFT Microsoft Corp 18.36%
3. V Visa Inc 4.35%
4. INTC Intel Corp 3.56%
5. MA Mastercard Inc 3.48%
6. CSCO Cisco Systems Inc 2.50%
7. NVDA NVIDIA Corp 2.49%
8. ADBE Adobe Inc 2.44%
9. PYPL PayPal Holdings Inc 2.22%
10. CRM Salesforce.Com Inc 2.01%
11. ORCL Oracle Corp 1.69%
12. ACN Accenture PLC 1.64%
13. AVGO Broadcom Inc 1.50%
14. IBM International Business Machines Corp 1.49%
15. TXN Texas Instruments Inc 1.48%

Number of Holdings: 316
Percent Assets in Top 15: 68.11%

Technology Select Sector SPDR® Fund (XLK)

Top 15 Holdings[3]
Expense ratio: .13%
Symbol/ Holding / % Assets

1. MSFT Microsoft Corp 21.91%
2. AAPL Apple Inc 20.15%
3. V Visa Inc 4.93%
4. INTC Intel Corp 4.04%
5. MA Mastercard Inc 3.90%
6. NVDA NVIDIA Corp 2.97%
7. CSCO Cisco Systems Inc 2.84%
8. ADBE Adobe Inc 2.77%
9. PYPL PayPal Holdings Inc 2.65%
10. CRM Salesforce.Com Inc 2.43%
11. ACN Accenture PLC 1.86%
12. ORCL Oracle Corp 1.80%
13. IBM International Business Machines Corp 1.69%
14. AVGO Broadcom Inc 1.69%
15. TXN Texas Instruments Inc 1.67%

Number of Holdings: 72
Percent Assets in Top 15: 77.30%

Technology Sector ETF comparison

Invesco QQQ Trust (QQQ) is based on the Nasdaq-100 Index and consists of all stocks in the Index.[4] Vanguard Information Technology (VGT) and Technology Select Sector SPDR Fund (XLK) invest in many of the same stocks, but neither fund considers Amazon a tech stock. Vanguard relegates Amazon to its Vanguard Consumer Discretionary (VCR) ETF.

So, if you invest in the VGT or XLK you may be in for a surprise when you discover you don't own Amazon. If that matters to you then you might consider Invesco QQQ Trust, which devotes 9.97% of its portfolio to Amazon[5].

Another major difference is that VGT and XLK don't own any Facebook or Google stock, and some would consider both of those tech companies. Instead, Vanguard includes both stocks in Vanguard Communication Services ETF (VOX) and SPDR includes them in Communication Services Select Sector SPDR Fund (XLC).

Because ETF providers have different criteria for what fits into the categories of tech, consumer discretionary, or communication services it's important for ETF investors who about the specific stocks in a fund to take a look at the holdings in advance: your definition of "tech" might be different than that of the ETF provider.

If VGT and XLK don't own any Alphabet, Amazon, or Facebook, what do they buy instead? At first glance, I notice that more than 18% of VGT and more than 20% of XLK is invested in both Microsoft and Apple. So, if you want to own stock in these two companies then you will own a lot with either VGT or XLK, but if you want to own Amazon you're out of luck, because neither own Amazon.

An investor should know which stocks are most important to them before buying a tech ETF. For example, I personally like Amazon, and if I were picking a tech fund I'd want to make sure it was an ETF like QQQ that owns Amazon.

The main "take-away" is you should *read the list of ETF holdings* before you buy so you'll know what you're getting. Just search for the fund ticker symbol followed by the word "holdings."

Despite these major allocation differences, you can see in the chart and table below that the returns of all three tech funds we have discussed are similar, with QQQ narrowly edging out the other funds over a 10 years.

Comparison of three technology ETFs. Source: Portfolio Visualizer April 8, 2020

Portfolio | Initial Balance | Final Balance | CAGR[6]

- Portfolio 1 - QQQ $10,000 $46,317 16.13%
- Portfolio 2- VGT $10,000 $43,259 15.36%
- Portfolio 3 - XLK $10,000 $41,479 14.89%

28

INTERNATIONAL ETFS

If you want to invest in international stocks you might want to consider one of these two funds. The first fund, VEA, focuses on companies based in developed markets, which are generally considered to be more stable. The second fund, VXUS, invests in stocks based in both developed and emerging markets.

There are many other ETF options available from other providers, but when I look carefully at the stocks they own I have noticed that each international or emerging markets fund owns pretty much the same stocks.

Both of these ETFs are offered by Vanguard and provide accurate tracking of their respective indexes and providing a way for investors to invest in developed and international markets at a low cost.

Vanguard Developed Markets (VEA)

Top 15 Holdings[1]
  Expense ratio: .05%
  Symbol/ Holding / % Assets

  1. NESN Nestle SA 1.92%

2. ROG Roche Holding AG 1.63%
3. 005930 Samsung Electronics Co Ltd 1.20%
4. NOVN Novartis AG 1.15%
5. 7203 Toyota Motor Corp 0.94%
6. AZN AstraZeneca PLC 0.92%
7. ASML ASML Holding NV 0.74%
8. SAP SAP SE 0.69%
9. SAN Sanofi SA 0.69%
10. 1299 AIA Group Ltd 0.68%
11. GSK GlaxoSmithKline PLC 0.66%
12. NOVO.B Novo Nordisk A/S 0.65%
13. HSBA HSBC Holdings PLC 0.64%
14. CSL CSL Ltd 0.57%
15. MC LVMH Moet Hennessy Louis Vuitton SE 0.57%

Number of Holdings: 1842
Percent Assets in Top 15: 13.65%

Vanguard International Stock (VXUS)

Top 15 Holdings[2]
Expense ratio: .08%
Symbol/ Holding / % Assets

1. BABA Alibaba Group Holding Ltd 1.69%
2. 700 Tencent Holdings Ltd 1.55%
3. NESN Nestle SA 1.46%
4. ROG Roche Holding AG 1.19%
5. 2330 Taiwan Semiconductor Manufacturing Co Ltd 1.11%
6. 005930 Samsung Electronics Co Ltd 0.95%
7. NOVN Novartis AG 0.86%
8. 7203 Toyota Motor Corp 0.69%
9. AZN AstraZeneca PLC 0.68%
10. ASML ASML Holding NV 0.56%
11. SAP SAP SE 0.52%

12. 1299 AIA Group Ltd 0.52%
13. SAN Sanofi SA 0.52%
14. NOVO.B Novo Nordisk A/S 0.50%
15. GSK GlaxoSmithKline PLC 0.49%

Number of Holdings: 1242
Percent Assets in Top 15: 13.28%

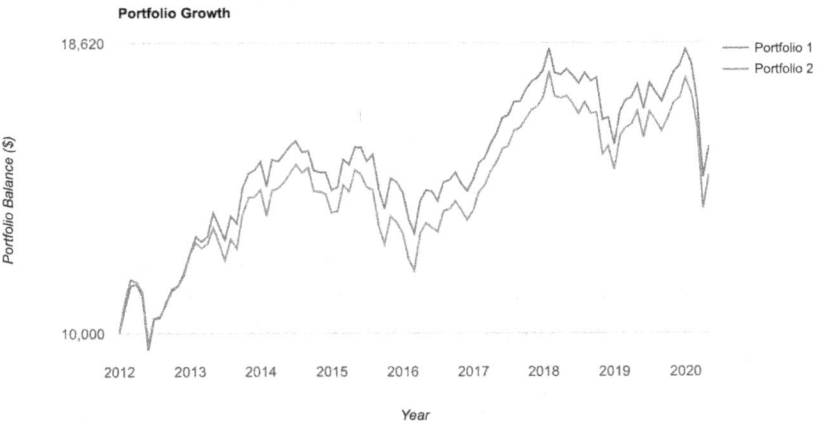

VEA vs. VXUS Source: Portfolio Visualizer 5/7/2020

Portfolio | Initial Balance | Final Balance | CAGR[3]

- Portfolio 1 - VEA $10,000 $14,932 4.93%
- Portfolio 2 - VXUS $10,000 $14,039 4.15%

The take-home lesson here is that both ETFs are well-diversified offerings, with each holding over 1,000 stocks[4]. VEA invests only in developed markets, while VXUS invests 76.8% in developed markets with 23.2% of the portfolio in emerging markets.[5]

29

PUTTING IT ALL TOGETHER

By now we've taken at many different ETFs, each with different characteristics. As we've pointed out, you can do fine owning just one of these funds, or diversifying into a few.

You might wonder what kind of conclusions you should draw. Should you just pick one ETF, two or three, or as many as 10?

There is no one answer about ETFs that will work for everyone. Your perfect solution will be different from another readers depending on how much volatility you can comfortably endure.

For example, much of the research points toward small-cap value stocks provide the best total return. In a 2016 article titled "Small-Cap Withdrawal Magic,"[1] William P. Bengen that investing 100% in small-cap stocks gave better results over most periods.

If this is true, and small-cap stocks have higher expected returns and provide the best safe withdrawal rates, why not go "all in" on small-cap stocks?

Bengen, who we discussed in the chapter about small-cap ETFs, explains why you might not want to invest everything in small caps.

On the Rational Reminder Podcast[2], Bengen explained, "They're a very volatile asset class. They've had years when they're down 65% - 70% and years they've been up 150%. So there's an enormous range, and not everyone can tolerate that kind of volatility in a portfolio... even if you know in the back of your mind it's going to work out over the long term."

So, while their returns can be among the best over the long term most investors would be terrified putting all or most of their money into only small-cap stocks.

This points to the usefulness of constructing a portfolio in which you spread your money into different investments.

How many boats are you trusting to deliver your money?

I recently read an article by Benjamin C. Halliburton titled, "How many boats are you trusting to deliver your money?"[3] which emphasized the importance of spreading your money into many different investments.

Halliburton observed that most people ride the ups and downs of the market, moving things around within their "investment boats" as needed while trying to stay afloat and navigate the choppy seas of the stock market — with their assets usually invested in US stocks and possibly US bonds.

He pointed out that if the stock market hits an iceberg, and investors are just moving items around in the same boat with their stocks, mutual funds, or ETFs, *"those assets are essentially all in the same boat and all go down together."*

The article explained that big institutions and wealthy families don't keep all their money in one boat. They split up their assets into multiple boats that are navigating different courses toward their destination.

So, I think you can picture many of the ETFs discussed in this book as different "boats" that can carry your assets toward your destination. If one of your investment "boats" is delayed or damaged, it's okay because your others are still on course. The wisdom of diversifying your assets is that you have your money spread along different routes in case one of your boats encounters stormy weather.

Some ETFs automatically dispatch your dollars into thousands of stocks and relieve you of the job of hiring many boats. For the adventurous investor who likes to choose their own boats, the 25 ETFs can help them power their portfolio by *tilting it in one direction* — essentially making small bets that certain asset classes will outperform others. By investing in biotech, health care, international, technology, or small-cap stocks an investor can highlight the market sectors they admire or understand most.

Ultimately, an investor may choose to optimize their portfolio's return, diversify into a variety of asset classes, or accomplish both by thoughtful ETF selection; there are many ways to guide your boats toward their destinations.

30

YOUR BIGGEST OBSTACLE

Why do some investors succeed while others fail?

There are many answers to this question, but in the end, I think it all comes down to *behavior*. It's our habits and the systems we cultivate that determine our success.

You will find that your biggest obstacle to investing is yourself. It's not so much the mistakes you make, but rather it is the mistakes of omission — the saving or investing you could do, but you postpone or avoid altogether.

So, which behaviors are most effective, and where can we learn them? Well, let me tell you a useful habit I discovered on my own.

After I graduated from college I moved to Seattle and started my freelance photography business. I was about 26 years old and I'd never invested in my life.

Soon after I started getting my first photo gigs I realized if I wanted to have any money in the future I couldn't depend on a pension or 401k (self-employed photographers don't get these). Yes, if I wanted to invest for my future I had to be resourceful.

I got started reading magazine articles, and soon after I started investing in a mutual fund, which is similar to an ETF but only trades at the end of the day. I needed to come up with a $1,000 deposit to open the account, and after that I invested $100 monthly. That turned out being pretty easy to do, as long as I saved money and didn't blow it on stuff I didn't need. Those early investments were the best decisions I ever made because they compounded over time. Today I'm sitting in the shade of trees I planted in my 20s.

Those early investments doubled, and then doubled again while I was out shooting photos and doing other things. You will also probably notice that the investments you make early in your life will be the best financial decisions you make; you'll only wish you started earlier or invested more!

Those monthly investments I made over several years were the easiest and best investments I ever made.

Even though it was easy for me to make those monthly investments, it took a little effort. I wrote a check every month, put it in an envelope and mailed it to the fund company. It's even easier to invest today with Internet brokers and investing apps. Today's tools make investing easy, which is good, according to the Nobel Prize-winning economist Richard Thaler, who said, "If you want people to do something, make it easy."

The key to getting started is making sure you put a good system in place that ensures you continue to invest at regular intervals through thick and thin—and especially through thin. It is during those times of fear and pessimism that stocks get cheap and you get the bargains that pave the way for strong future returns.

Your First Steps

To get better at ETF investing, as with anything in life, you have to experiment. It involves trying, failing, and learning from your mistakes. Fortunately, the cost of an ETF investment can be as small as the cost of one share, so you don't have to risk much at all when you're starting out. Even if you don't have enough money to buy a whole share of an ETF, you can still buy a fractional share.[1]

Fractional shares let you buy a slice of your favorite ETFs based on how much you want to invest, so even if you don't want to buy one share for $175 you can buy a fraction of it based on how many dollars you want to invest.

What are some behavior tricks to help you get started?

Starting is the hardest part of investing

I was listening to the CarTalk podcast the other day — these are "best of" recordings from a show that used to be on the radio. People call in with car problems, and the hosts — Click and Clack — try to solve them. Someone called in and said he wanted to buy a car, but he had two problems: as a newly minted PhD he admitted to having no money and no common sense. The podcast hosts asked him what he got his PhD in, and when he said, "geography" the hosts howled with laughter: "Isn't that pretty much *closed*? I mean, *what the hell's happening*?"

Their point is that most of the planet has been mapped out; there's nothing left to discover. By the same token, investing as a science is largely a solved problem. Sure, there are people poking around the edges and trying to squeeze a tiny bit of return with some new strategy, but there's nothing innovative happening in the investment world.

Yes, we have markets for cryptocurrencies, gold, silver, ETFs, mutual funds, stocks, and other investments; these are different things to invest or gamble on, but *nothing new under the sun*. Investors understand that the prices of these assets fluctuate and have figured out ways to gain and lose money investing and trading them. People have traded these assets for centuries and this will continue in the future, and *we understand the science* of investing in markets.

While the science of investing is pretty much solved, *investor behavior* is a new field that raises questions that have not been answered. The biggest question I can think of is why some people take naturally to investing without much effort while others struggle to get started and keep to a schedule.

Why do some investors succeed while others fail?

Many people with no formal financial training successfully invest, while others with advanced degrees don't understand investing or have never started.

I believe that successful investment does not require early education (high school or college), but learning how to invest "just in time" — when a person needs to use the information in real life.

For example, I lived many years without knowing anything about buying a house, getting it inspected, or the importance of low mortgage rates. Then, when I finally decided to buy a house I was a sponge for housing and mortgage information.

If I had learned about buying a home years earlier I would have likely forgotten everything because it wasn't relevant to me and I would not have had a reason to remember all the data and lessons others might have shared with me.

If this is true, then educating people about how to invest *when they realize they need to grow their money* might be *more effective than teaching them about compound interest in high school* years before they'll need to understand it.

Why don't people save?

The simple fact that 58% of Americans have less than $1,000 in savings shows how many people are poorly equipped for emergencies, not to mention having no plan to avoid being broke when they retire.[2]

So how can people learn to save and invest? Is it even worth teaching investing in high school? Many of the lessons we learn in school are forgotten long before we need to remember them. On the subject of teaching investing in school, Thaler, the Nobel Prize-winning economist said, "The real point is not whether we should be teaching high school students about interest rates and compound interest because obviously, we should — the question is whether we think it's going to solve any problems, *and the answer is that it won't.*"

Thaler said that sometimes he will ask an audience how much they remember from their high school chemistry class. "If they're not a chemist, it's basically nothing," he said. "So, you know, if we teach people about compound interest, great, will it help them 20 years later when they're ready to buy a home? Probably not."

Teach when the student is ready

So, if early education about investing won't work, how do we teach people so they learn just in time? Is there a period when students are most receptive to learning, and when that time arrives, how does the teacher know?

I can't answer these questions for everyone, but I can tell you that I had no interest at all to learn about investing when I was in high school or college. In fact, I remember seeing students at my college carrying around copies of the *Wall Street Journal*, and I thought it was the most useful newspaper I'd ever seen: it didn't even have photographs! I was curious why they were carrying those newspapers around campus until I learned that they were required reading for an economics class.

My point is that the *Wall Street Journal* seemed completely useless to me as a 19-year-old college student, and I never read a single page of the newspaper. Today I light up when I see the journal and admire the quality writing and in-depth coverage of investing, money, and markets.

The reality is that investing seemed irrelevant to me when I was in college; I remember being curious about the stock symbols and numbers in the pages of the financial section of the newspaper, but they seemed like a foreign language.

I majored in biology and graduated from college without taking a single business, economics, or math class. I decided that I would become a photographer, and didn't have the slightest clue that investing would eventually be helpful in life.

However, later in life when I set out on my own and became a professional photographer, suddenly earning some dollars and putting them in the bank became a big deal. But soon my optometrist would ask me a question that would change my perception of investing forever.

My optometrist asked me a question

After I graduated from college I started working as a newspaper photographer. I was what they call a "stringer," which means you're a journalist or photographer who has no contract or formal employment but goes on assignments as needed. I was earning $35 per photoshoot, which was not much at all, and I had no formal plan for saving or investing.

I remember a visit with my optometrist after I graduated from college. He and I got along well, and during one conversation he asked, *"Have you ever thought of putting money in an account where it could get you a better return than what you get in a checking account?"*

It was a simple question, and I told him that I'd never considered it, but I wanted to learn. The truth is I would probably never have thought to invest if a helpful friend hadn't thought to ask me that question. Up until that point in my life, nobody had ever spoken to me about investing; not my mother, father, teacher, or friend.

I didn't know the first thing about stocks or mutual funds, and would probably never have searched out information about them on my own. If my optometrist never asked me that question I may never have started investing, and this book would not exist.

My optometrist asked me the question "just in time" for me to get curious and start searching for answers. In my direct experience, the teaching needed to happen when I was hungry for the information, not years earlier when I could not yet envision how the lesson could apply to my life.

One photocopied article

My optometrist gave me a photocopy of a multi-page magazine article about investing in mutual funds with a Post-It note attached.

"Read this and then you'll know more about investing than a broker. Then we can discuss it further."

So, I think the best teacher is one with useful information prepared to present it when the student is ready. Early in life a student may not yet need the lesson, and if you wait too long it may be too late: "just in time" education is useful.

Thaler emphasizes that this is the secret to teaching. "Just-in-time education and simple products," he said. "Make it simple."[3].

31

ACTIVE MANAGERS CHOOSE INDEX INVESTING

Richard Thaler won the Nobel Prize in economics for his work in behavioral economics, which he describes as "economics about humans.[1]"

One surprising discovery I made while writing this book is that although Thaler himself co-founded a mutual fund company specializing in actively managed funds,[2] he chooses passively managed index funds for his retirement account. Thaler said, "Everyone should invest their money either in index funds or in funds managed by Fuller and Thaler,"[3] he said with a smile.

Thaler said, "I'm in the active fund management business, although my retirement income — which is from a set of funds that the university selects — is all in index funds."

If the Nobel Prize winner in Economics invests in index funds, I think it makes sense to take that into account when making your own decisions. I'm not saying that it's the best approach for everyone, but I think Thaler's choice suggests that he seeks to own asset classes, but he doesn't want to pay fees to investment managers.

I want to point out that when Thaler says he invests in "index funds" he could be talking about old school "index funds"[4] or ETFs that invest in an index. These are just two vehicles for investing; the mutual fund has been around longer, and the ETF is a more recent product. It doesn't matter which one you use to invest because the underlying stocks are the same.

Automated investing with index funds

There is *one thing you don't get with an ETF* that you can get with index funds: the *ability to automate periodic investments*. This process, also known as recurring investment, allows you to invest a specified amount of money every month, or at any interval you choose.

This is an excellent system for anyone who wants to invest regularly but *knows they might not remember to do so*. To set up automatic investments you link your bank account to an index fund account and select a dollar amount and interval at which you would like to invest.

The automated feature makes investing *simple*. It is the perfect way to sidestep one error of human behavior — our tendency to forget.

You can't do recurring investments using ETFs because they are traded during the day on the stock market. Because prices fluctuate throughout the day, the purchase price for an ETF is variable and it would be impossible for a brokerage firm to know when to buy your shares.

Because index mutual funds are priced once each day (at a price determined after markets close), a fund company has only one price at which to sell you shares.

This *once-a-day pricing* makes index mutual funds more useful for "set-it-and-forget-it" investors who want to have the investments made throughout the year without ever having to think about it. ETFs are still useful to investors, especially those who want to trade their own shares and don't need automated investments.

If you like the idea of automated investments you might find index mutual funds more useful than ETFs. There is nothing wrong with investing in them, even though this book focuses on ETFs.

There is a lot to love about index mutual funds — especially the ability to automate your investments.

If this interests you, then check out the Vanguard S&P 500 Index Fund (VFIAX), Fidelity 500 Index Fund (FXAIX), or Schwab S&P 500 Index Fund (SWPPX). These funds have different minimum initial investments, low fees, and they all permit recurring investments.

32

IMPROVING INVESTOR BEHAVIOR

Daniel Kahneman and Richard Thaler share their theories about the ways that humans are apt to engage in a number of fallacies and human errors that drive harmful behaviors.

What are these biases, and how can we seek workarounds?

I've never found a practical book about investing that helped readers improve their *behavior*, so I'm taking it upon myself to provide this information to readers.

You can improve behavior:

1. Plan to *pay yourself first* and put some money in a savings reserve. Once you have built your reserve you can start to invest the rest.
2. Promise yourself that you will tune out distracting financial news and not feel you have to market time by jumping in and out of the market.

The first item ensures you remember to invest before you spend money on other things you may not need, and the second helps you to continue investing while ignoring the state of the economy, politics, and the stock market.

I want to give you "just enough" information so you can use it, but not so much that it's overwhelming.

How can you make sure you start saving money now so you can start investing for your future? Can you pick a start day for yourself and stick to it?

33

A BEHAVIOR TRICK

I'd like to share with you one *behavior trick* I used to help me muster the courage to invest in stocks when everyone else was freaking out during the COVID-19 pandemic.

Fear was at an all-time high, news articles popped up several times a day with headlines fanning the flames of fear, talking about the deadly virus, and various ways to protect yourself.

The stock apps on my phone were covered in red. Stocks were down 5%, 7%, 11%, or more for days on end. Markets plunged day after day with no end in sight.

Everywhere you looked people were losing their minds. Warren Buffett put his finger on the fear gripping the world during his virtual presentation of the Berkshire Hathaway Annual Meeting when he said, "Fear is the most contagious disease you can imagine."

What was the trick I used to invest? Instead of fixating on fear like other investors, *I thought about how much stocks would be worth in three, five, or 10 years. I visualized the future* and how investing in ETFs in March of 2020 would be a smart investment when viewed many years later.

This chart shows the performance of stocks in the S&P 500 index over the past 90 years, with recessions shown by shaded areas. Despite the Great Depression, two world wars, the Dot.com bubble, terrorist attacks, and the financial crisis, the stock market has continued its ascent. I keep this graph in mind to give me courage during times when others are fearful. If you keep focused on the long-term you can keep cool when others are losing their minds. Source: Standard & Poor's.

The simple mindset shift from *today* to the *future* helps me buy stocks during times of crisis. I know that most problems with the stock market and the economy will pass, and people around the world will recover and prosper, and the US economy will continue climbing upward, and the stock market will follow. As the philosopher, Spinoza said, *"You must look at things in the aspect of eternity."*[1]

I have no way of knowing if markets will go down or up in the short term, so I just divide my cash into a few chunks and *invest at intervals*. That way I don't invest everything at once, and I can spread out my investments over time.

At the foundation of this behavior is my belief that *if you buy a group of excellent businesses when they're cheap and hold them for a long time, it's almost impossible to lose money.*

One thing I like about ETFs is that they make it easy to buy a group of stocks instead of buying just one. When the markets were falling quickly I knew I wanted to invest, but I couldn't decide quickly which stocks to buy: Adobe, Alaska Airlines, Berkshire Hathaway, Chevron, Costco, Disney, Fiat Chrysler, General Motors, Ford, Jet Blue, Microsoft, Nike, or, Simons Property Group, or Starbucks?

There were all of these stocks suddenly really cheap, but which ones should I buy? If I tried to pick one I would get "analysis paralysis" and not buy anything.

So, I decided to buy Vanguard S&P 500 ETF (VOO) in March as stocks crashed. It was the first ETF I ever bought, and I reached for it because it was a simple choice. I bought shares on different days because I did not know which day would offer the lowest prices. Soon after I added Vanguard Small-Cap ETF (VB) to my investments. I saw this ETF falling rapidly in price and I knew if I bought it cheap everything would work out well in the long term.

This mindset of buying great companies and owning them for many years into the future instead of fixating on the current atmosphere of fear was helpful. I hope you will find this trick of thinking long-term to be useful too.

So now that you know some good ETFs to consider, and the best behavior hacks to keep you on track, how do you plan for your future success?

34

PAY YOURSELF FIRST

Have you ever heard of Parkinson's Law? It's a law of human behavior that states, "Work expands to fill the time available for its completion."

The more time you have to complete something, the longer it will take you to finish it. It's the classic procrastination trap, and it's the reason most homework gets done the night before it's due (or right before class).

Well, this same law applies to money. You will buy more things until you use up your whole paycheck. No matter how much money you earn, you'll find new and inventive ways to spend it, whether on dinner out with your friends, that cool pair of sneakers, or some late-night Amazon Prime shopping.

I would like to give credit to a YouTube content creator named Rose, who has an excellent channel[1]. Rose was once a financial analyst and she shares many useful ideas and advice for investors on how to save and invest. I came across Rose's video: "Budgeting for Beginners: 8 Places Your Money Needs to Go."[2] It is full of useful insights and practical tips, and I share them with you below. If you enjoy YouTube videos I think you'll enjoy her channel: Investing With Rose.

THE ETF INVESTOR

Rose's video brought up the idea of Parkinson's law, and how if we aren't careful we'll spend whatever money we have on things we like or want, but this behavior means there's nothing left to invest after we've blown it on non-essential things.

She also gives specific advice on paying yourself first so that you get to keep some of your money and put it in an emergency reserve fund, and into savings and investing accounts. I think it's great advice, and I've adjusted it slightly for this book — I provide five ways to pay yourself first instead of eight, and I like ETFs currently while Rose prefers index funds.

If you prefer index funds there are many options available. Whether you choose an ETF or index fund is up to you: they're both simple ways to invest for your future.

Five ways to pay yourself first

1. Set up a cash reserve. This is an automated, recurring transfer from the checking account into a savings account for emergencies. You could also call this your emergency fund or a savings reserve. The point it that you want to have money set aside to pay for food, rent, car repairs, or any other essentials in case of emergency. You will not be touching this money (only adding to the account) and ideally this savings account will pay interest. Start with $100 if you can, and add more if possible. Your goal with this emergency fund is to help you to stay out of debt and not have to put unexpected expenses on your credit card. So, when your car breaks down or your pet gets sick, instead of stressing about how you're going to pay for it you can just dip into your emergency fund.

Ideally, you want to have three to six months of living expenses set aside in your emergency fund. That takes time to accomplish, but $1,000 is a good starter emergency fund and will put you ahead of the 58% of Americans who don't even have $1,000 saved to cover emergencies. The prospect of a pandemic or any economic hardship where your earning power evaporates should be a strong incentive to start building an emergency fund now.

There are many options for your emergency savings fund. If you want to go for pure savings account you can look at Ally Bank Online Savings, Betterment's Cash Reserve savings account, Capital One 360 Performance Savings, or Marcus by Goldman Sachs. You want to make sure you're getting a high annual percentage yield (also known as the APY, search a few banks to make sure you're getting a high rate), no monthly fees, and no minimums to open or maintain your high-yield savings account.

If you already have a brokerage account at Fidelity, Schwab, or Vanguard you can use one of their money market accounts to park your emergency cash. Just make sure the APY is competitive with the savings accounts mentioned above. Some brokerages pay a very low APY for their "sweep" money market accounts because many customers don't notice - they get to use your cash and you get little in return, so make sure you're getting a good rate, which is about 1.5% -1.9% at the time of this writing. These rates fluctuate, and I just want to make sure you get the highest interest rate for your savings account as possible - why not? It's free money!

2. *Have your paycheck deposited into your checking account.* Go for one that does not charge a monthly fee. Fidelity and Schwab both offer checking account options. You want to get make sure you get some interest on your checking account balance, and steer clear of any monthly fees. Make sure there is no required minimum balance, no overdraft fees, and the account is FDIC insured. Many checking accounts pay interest, so do some research to find out which ones do pay interest and get a feel for which checking account you like most.

3. *Contribute to your 401(K).* Automate contributions to your 401(K) if your employer provides you with the option. You can contribute a fixed percentage of your paycheck (up to a full employer match) to your 401(K). Matching contributions are free money: take it.

4. *Fully fund your Roth IRA.* This is a type of tax-advantaged investment account that will help you save and invest for retirement. The reason you may want to consider a Roth is that you fund it with "afte-tax" money, and it is the only investment account that does not

require payment of taxes after you retire (because you funded it with money you already paid taxes on).

You can open an IRA at several financial firms like: Fidelity, Schwab, and Vanguard. Consider contributing $500 a month as an automatic monthly transfer so you don't have to think about it because that gets you to $6,000 a year[3], which is the annual contribution limit. Even if you don't have $500 a month to contribute it makes sense to make some contribution, even if it's just $50 or $100 a month. There's nothing worse than ending up old and broke: one main benefit of a Roth IRA is that when you withdraw money in retirement you pay no deferred taxes.

5. *Invest* - I originally started investing with mutual funds, then I graduated to index fund investing, and now I invest in both stocks and ETFs. I still hold some of my early mutual funds and let them compound in value. I just like ETFs for their low cost and ease of use.

Your ultimate choice of investment vehicle is a personal choice. This book focuses on ETFs, but there are many other ways to invest, including index funds like those mentioned in an earlier chapter.

Build a cash reserve

We've already touched on building an emergency reserve, and how you can put yourself in a good position by building a reserve to pay for life's emergencies: car problems, medical bills, or food and rent.

Here's a letter that I think you'll enjoy, it was sent by Warren Buffett's grandfather Ernest to his uncle Fred and Fred's wife, Catherine.

Dear Fred & Catherine:

Over a period of a good many years I have known a great many people who at some time or another have suffered in various ways simply because they did not have ready cash. I have known people how have had to sacrifice some of their holdings in order to have money that was necessary at that time.

For a good many years your grandfather kept a certain amount of money where he could put his hands on it in very short notice.

For a number of years I have made it a point to keep a reserve, should some occasion come up where I would need money quickly, without disturbing the money that I have in my business. There have been a couple occasions when I found it very convenient to go to this fund.

Thus, I feel that everyone should have a reserve. I hope it never happens to you, but the chances are that some day you will need money, and need it badly, and with this thought in view, I started a fund by placing $200.00 in an envelope, with your name on it, when you were married. Each year I added something to it, until there is now $1000.00 in the fund.

Ten years have elapsed since you were married, and this fund is now completed.

It is my wish that you place this envelope in your safety deposit box, and keep it for the purpose that it was created for. Should the time come when you need part, I would suggest that you use as little as possible, and replace it as soon as possible.

You might feel that this should be invested and bring you an income. Forget it — the mental satisfaction of having $1000.00 laid away where you can put your hands on it, is worth more than what interest it might bring, especially if you have the investment in something that you could not realize on quickly.

If in after years you feel this has been a good idea, you might repeat it with your own children.

For your information, I might mention that there has never been a Buffett who ever left a very large estate, but there has never been one that did not leave something. They never spent all they made, but always saved part of what they made, and it has all worked out pretty well.

This letter is being written at the expiration of ten years after you were married.

— Ernest Buffett "Dad"

I share this letter with you because I think it will drive home the importance of keeping a certain amount of money laid away where you can put your hands on it. Having this reserve gives you peace of mind when the unexpected arrives. I had a reserve in place when the Coronavirus pandemic hit in 2020 and I'm glad I did.

Each person reading this book will probably have some unexpected expense at some time in their life, and you'll be thankful if you take Warren Buffett's grandfather's advice and set up a reserve.

This notion is probably something you've heard of before, and I share the letter because I think it shows that every generation in history has had its challenges, and keeping some money where you can get to it in emergencies can provide mental satisfaction.

35

THINK ABOUT RIP VAN WINKLE

Individual investors have a knack for buying high and selling low. Economist Richard Thaler said, "There was a study done of long-term investors in mutual funds, and they underperformed the funds they owned by about 1.5%, purely because of the timing of their trades.[1]"

In other words, investors are screwing themselves out of better returns through human errors that drive them to buy when markets are high and sell when markets are low. Good investing is not about being a genius, but it requires the right temperament to tune out the noise and not react out of fear as a result of whatever is happening in the stock market.

Thaler says that whatever they do, investors should not be glued to cable financial news networks that are on 24/7.

"Think about Rip Van Winkle," Thaler said. "You know, suppose he is an economist, so he has rational expectations, he knows he's about to go to sleep for 20 years…and calls his broker and says, *'put it all in equities!'* How's he gonna sleep? Fine! There's never been a 20 year period when equities didn't go up or didn't outperform bonds, so he's gonna sleep very well."

The less attention you pay, the more money you'll have

Now compare that behavior to someone who's glued to their phone's stock app or financial news stations all the time, and they're going to freak out when they see stocks are down 5% or more in a day. They have a reaction based on fear. They may feel the need to *do something*, and most often they'll make a mistake.

I follow several YouTubers, and during the wild stock swings that have occurred during the pandemic, they have announced publicly that they're either buying tons of stocks or selling and going to 100% cash.

These YouTubers have between 80,000 and 450,000 followers who are glued to their videos every day. Social media platforms have become the financial news networks for a new generation of investors, and financial trading apps on phones have made it very easy to buy and sell stocks any time of day with no commissions.

The comments under the videos suggest that viewers are buying and selling stocks daily. It's become a mixture of sports, video games, and casino gambling.

"The less attention people pay the better they're gonna sleep, and ironically the more money they'll have," Thaler said. Keep those words in the front of your mind as you invest. Remember that *frequent trading a lot does not increase your chances of success*, and it often works against you.

Now that we've looked at human behavior, let's take a look behind the scenes. Have you ever wondered about the "secret sauce" that makes ETFs unique?

36

CREATION AND REDEMPTION

You can drive a car for your whole life without ever understanding how an engine works, and you can invest in ETFs without understanding creation and redemption.

Yet, sometimes you get curious and want to take a look "under the hood" and figure out what makes things work.

Any essential book about ETFs *must* describe creation and redemption, and leaving this mechanism out would be a gaping omission. You, as the reader, are free to skip this chapter, and you are forgiven in advance. This is technical stuff, and you don't have to know the details to trade ETFs.

But, for those adventurous souls who like to dive in and get granular, let's take a look at what's going behind the scenes. The creation and redemption process is at the core of what makes ETFs so simple.

Much of the information below was gathered from "The Rational Reminder" podcast during which he described the process of creation and redemption. ETF expert David Nadig was a guest on the podcast, and he gave an excellent summary of the process that made it easy to grasp[1].

In Nadig's YouTube video titled, "ETF Creation & Redemption,[2]" he does a good job of describing the mechanism. I've summarized the most important parts below, and I give credit to Mr. Nadig for the explanations while taking full responsibility for any inaccuracies.

Creation and redemption are truly the "secret sauce" behind ETFs: the invisible process that provides transparency, tax efficiency, and low costs. It's also a detailed process that takes some time to explain. For some people in the ETF business who have to explain this process over and over, it must be a tedious process. Nadig said, "I feel like if I have to tell somebody how creation and redemption work one more time, I'm going to take a spoon to my eyeballs[3]."

Let's first look at mutual funds

We can understand the process of creation and redemption by comparing it to a mutual fund, which is an investment that some readers already understand. With a mutual fund, investors pool their money to invest it together.

Instead of investing in stocks, if we decide to pool our money with a bunch of friends we can invest together.

For example, five of us can each contribute $10,000 to the pool, and in exchange each gets 100 shares worth $100 each.

Now that we've put that money in a pool, we decide to hire somebody to manage it for us. Let's say they do a fantastic job, and they double the amount of money in the pool. So it goes from being a $50,000 investment to a $100,000 investment. Now we all still have 100 shares in the pool, but each share is now worth twice as much money — $200 each.

The beauty of this system — of keeping track of everything in shares — is that when one of you wants to leave — *you can*. You turn in your 100 shares to the mutual fund pool, you get back your $20,000, and the pool is now worth $80,000.

Now, let's imagine your friend Pete wants to get in. Well, he shows up with his $10,000, but the shares are now worth $200, so he only gets 50 shares back. The pool now has $90,000 and things just keep chugging along.

That's the beauty of a mutual fund: it keeps track of everything for you but still lets you access a common pool with economies of scale. Now, most of us don't start a mutual fund with our friends; instead, we buy mutual fund shares that already exist.

There are a couple of ways to do that. You can either go to your broker and buy 100 shares of a mutual fund, or you can go directly to the fund company and buy 100 shares from them. *But you can't make any transactions during the day because no mutual fund transactions occur until after the stock market closes.*

At the close, the fund does a little math: it adds up the value of all its assets: stock, bonds, cash, etc., and then divides it by the number of shares that exist. It comes up with a "Net Asset Value" or NAV, a dollar value per share. And then it lets you buy or sell shares at that price.

For example, if you want to buy mutual fund shares they'll take your $10,000, they'll sell you 100 shares, and then tomorrow morning they'll put your money to work buying assets according to the fund's mandate.

The important thing to keep in mind is that mutual fund share prices are based on the value of assets held by the pool and the number of shares that exist. These prices are calculated once a day after the market closes.

The take-home lesson: *When you transact mutual fund shares you buy or sell from a common pool.*

ETFs don't use a pool

An ETF is exactly like a mutual fund with one difference: *you and I don't give our money directly to the pool.*

We have somebody in the middle called an "authorized participant," and their job is to go buy up all the stocks that the pool needs to be fully invested. An authorized participant is an institutional investor who makes new shares (a creation), or does the opposite and gets ride of those shares (a redemption).

Authorized participants do all the hard work of buying and selling those stocks in the marketplace every day in exchange for ETF

THE ETF INVESTOR

shares. Those shares are available for investors to trade on an exchange.

The mechanism to buy an ETF is the same as that used to buy stock on your brokerage website or app. You place your ETF order with the broker, that broker gets the best price for you in the market, and they hand those shares back to you — *just like you were buying a stock*. That could happen at 9 am, 11:05 am, 2:17 pm, or it could happen at the close. No matter what time of day you buy or sell your shares, you don't have to wait 'till the end of the day like you would with a mutual fund. With an ETF you are interacting with the market in real-time.

The take-home lesson: *When you trade shares of an ETF you're interacting with the market.*

How does ETF money get invested?

If I'm buying shares through my broker, or an app on my phone, or from other participants in the market, how in the world does my money get invested with the ETF company?[4]

That's where the creation and redemption process kicks in. The authorized participant—they're the only ones "authorized" to make or get rid of new shares of the ETF—is your liaison with the ETF company. They take a shopping list and go out buying stocks.

Creation

How do authorized participants fill the shopping list? Well, the ETF company gives them that shopping list of stocks that says, "*Here are all the things that we want to own.*" So, the authorized participant goes out to the marketplace, and they buy all the stocks on that shopping list: Adobe, Amazon, CRISPR, Dropbox, Editas, Microsoft, NVIDIA, Micron, Microsoft, Square, and Zoom — and they hand all those stocks over to the ETF company. In return, the ETF company wraps those stocks in a package and hands those new shares of the ETF back to the authorized participant. That's called a *create*.

165

Redemption

Now, redemption works in the opposite direction. Let's say the authorized participant has a whole bunch of shares of the ETF that they don't want anymore. Well, they just hand those shares over to the ETF company, and the package is unwrapped and the authorized participant gets back all the stocks on that shopping list: Adobe, Amazon, CRISPR, Dropbox, Editas, Microsoft, NVIDIA, Micron, Microsoft, Square, and Zoom—whatever it was they wanted — which the authorized participant can then go sell on the open market. That's called a *redeem*.

Now, the interesting question is, *why would somebody bother doing all that?*

It all comes down to greed.

On Wall Street everybody's greedy, and those authorized participants make money because most of the time they can sell an ETF share in the open market for a penny or two more than it cost them to create it by buying up all the underlying shares.

Profit drives the process

The profit motive is what keeps ETFs trading very close to their fair value. As soon as they get away from fair value, there's *more money for those authorized participants to make,* and there's competition, so they tend to only let ETF share prices drift by a few pennies.

Let's imagine the authorized participant is watching this particular ETF like a wolf watches a rabbit. They see the ETF is trading for $227 a share, and then they're looking at what the basket's worth: all the stocks they'd need to buy on the shopping list to make an ETF share. As long as those things are equal, the authorized participant is not going to do anything. There's no profit opportunity for them.

But imagine there's so much demand for this ETF that its price goes sky high—it trades for a premium. All of a sudden people are willing to pay $227.10 for that basket *which is only worth $227.*

Well, the authorized participant notices that, and they make a

THE ETF INVESTOR

simple transaction. They sell the ETF at that inflated $227.10 price, and then simultaneously they go out and buy all the things on the shopping list: Adobe, Amazon, CRISPR, Dropbox, Editas, Microsoft, NVIDIA, Micron, Microsoft, Square, and Zoom, etc. The net result is quite good for the ETF because the authorized participant is now a seller of the ETF, pushing its price down, and they're a buyer of all those underlying stocks, pulling those prices up.

And they'll keep buying and selling like that until they've equalized out the price. So the ETF may now be worth $227.01, but that's what the basket of stocks is worth too. So it's great for the ETF, but it's also great for the authorized participant because they were able to buy a basket of securities for $227 and then sell the ETF for $227.10. They made $.10 on every share, knowing at the end of the day they can just deliver that basket and get the shares that they've already sold to the market.

Profits on the way down

Creation and redemption work great in the other direction too. Imagine lots of people want to sell this ETF: there's some bad news, it's fallen out of favor, and things are not looking good for that ETF. Well, everybody starts dumping this ETF and it starts trading a little below fair value. Now it's trading for $226.90 even though the basket is still worth $227. So the authorized participant does the same thing they did for creation, they just do it in reverse: they go out there and buy a whole block of those cheap shares at $226.90 and simultaneously they go sell all the underlying holdings of the ETF.

The math for the authorized participant works the same way: they've managed to make $.10 on that trade and they put buying pressure on the ETF pulling it back up closer to fair value, and they put selling pressure on those stocks, pushing them down to where the market wants them to be.

So again, we get equalization of the prices, and the authorized participant makes a small profit. This kind of transaction is known as an "in-kind transfer." No cash changes hands between the ETF issuer and the authorized participant unless cash is on the shopping list. Instead, we're changing one set of securities for another. We're exchanging shares of the fund for shares of the stocks that it owns. It works that way for bonds, swaps, and commodities futures. In-kind transactions are the basic mechanism that make ETFs work.

Tax efficiency

One of the big bonuses we get from this process is tax efficiency because nothing has been sold, there has been no gain or loss booked on behalf of the fund. When the authorized participant shows up with a redemption, the ETF gets to decide which shares, of all the shares that it owns, it wants to give to the authorized participant.

It's no surprise that the ETF company chooses the shares with the lowest cost basis, in other words, the shares that if they were sold would generate capital gains. Over time, this means that *the ETF is very unlikely to pay a capital gains distribution* because it has *constantly pushed out those low basis shares* to the authorized participant every time there's been a redemption.

Let's talk about some of the great things that *aren't* happening with ETFs that happen with mutual funds and other investments that require a lot of investor hand-holding. First, the ETF sponsor doesn't need to be involved with the investor at all — they don't have to keep shareholder records or provide statements, they don't have to handle customer service phone calls or keep track of my mailing address, and they can't charge ETF investors a sales load because there is nobody in the middle except a broker, and lately almost all ETF trades are commission-free.

In his detailed explanation of ETF creation and redemption[5] Nadig says that the process ensures that the issuer is always operating at scale because they don't have to worry about making small transactions like a $500 creation because the authorized participant can only create and redeem in blocks of at least 50,000 shares. This means that the ETF portfolio manager doesn't need to keep cash on hand to sell if a shareholder suddenly shows up with a big redemption.

Remember, a big redemption doesn't require a portfolio manager to sell a bunch of stocks or other assets, it just means that the authorized participant hands over a basket of securities that matches everything in the fund provider's shopping list.

Another benefit of in-kind redemptions is they give the portfolio manager the flexibility to re-balance the portfolio if stocks get added to or removed from the underlying index.

Nadig explained that if one stock is getting kicked out of the S&P 500 index and another stock is being added, then today the authorized participant can make the redemption basket have all the stocks that are leaving the index, and the creation basket has all the stocks that are added.

"When you think about it, most of the things that are great about ETFs come from this creation redemption process," Nadig said.

Low cost, tax efficient & transparent

ETFs are low cost because the creation and redemption mechanism *removes transaction costs, shareholder servicing costs*, and *transfer agency costs*. ETFs are cheaper to run, which means that they're usually cheaper for investors.

When we talk about ETFs being tax-efficient, you can see that *the creation and redemption mechanism is why ETFs are tax-efficient*. Creation and redemption is smooth and flexible, and by using in-kind transfer it washes potential capital gains away.

ETF transparency is at the heart of the creation redemption process because the authorized participant *needs to know exactly what's on the shopping list*, and more often than not, that's the whole portfolio. So, as an investor you don't have to wait until the end of the quarter to see what's in the fund: the list is updated every day.

The authorized participant gets to see that list of holdings, and you get to see it too. All you have to do is Google the ETF ticker symbol and the word "holdings" and it will be one of the top results.

As for liquidity, creation and redemption *attract liquidity providers* because there's an opportunity to make money by trading whenever there's a discrepancy between the price the ETFs selling at and the cost to buy the underlying securities. Authorized participants aren't doing this for fun, they're doing it because they can make beaucoup bucks providing liquidity to ETF investors.

Creation and redemption are at the core of what makes ETFs so simple. "Without the creation redemption mechanism we couldn't have fair prices, we couldn't have this great tax efficiency, we probably wouldn't have the breadth of products that we have,"Nadig said.[6]

The creation redemption mechanism underpins much of what makes ETFs remarkable investments.

37

PLAN FOR SUCCESS

Here are a few ways you can increase your chances for ETF investing success.

It's impossible to time the stock market. Instead of trying to pick the perfect time to buy ETFs, one approach is to write down a plan that you will follow.

I write things in a journal.

How to make your plan:

1. Make a step-by-step plan
2. Tell other people about your plans
3. Make a system to invest at regular intervals
4. Think about the good things that will happen if you progress and reward yourself for taking action
5. Record your progress (e.g., in a journal or on a chart)

I've modified these steps from a list in a book called "59 Seconds[1]" by Richard Wiseman. I found the whole book, especially the chapter on motivation, full of useful ideas.

Keeping an investment journal keeps me creative and reflective. I like getting ideas out of my head and onto paper; there's something about writing that brings mental clarity.

If you haven't tried writing in a journal you might find part of your mind opens up and discovers new ideas just by writing, doodling, making a step-by-step plan, or recording your progress.

Get early wins

Sometimes it's hard to feel you're making progress without some small, early wins. What I mean by that is just feeling like you are on the right track and advancing toward your goals.

Your goals may be to build an emergency fund, save to buy a used car, pay for school or buy a house. Maybe you want to invest enough money so you can retire early and not have to worry about working forever. These big goals can take years to accomplish, but you'll never progress toward them until you start, and writing them down is the first step that primes the pump to start things flowing.

Once you have a small, early win you will get a dopamine hit and that will give you some positive reinforcement that you're on the right track. I think that often people who never start something just get stuck in a circuit of thinking and re-thinking; it gets stuck in a loop of thinking but never springs free into action.

I think people get stuck in these loops of inaction because they never get the quick rush of an early win and the feeling of progress when you know you're on the right track.

If you start putting $100 into your emergency fund every month, or you decide to buy one share of an ETF, you will break out of that *overthinking* mode and get into *action* mode.

Once you start taking action and getting early wins you build mental momentum. You start feeling good, and those fears you had (often unrealistic) dissolve when you realize they were illusions and not reality.

One decision leads to the next. Innovating means trying something new, and there's always going to be some fear of making mistakes. But, just remember that if you make a small investment then you're not risking it all, you're being smart. And if you make a mistake you can always learn from it and try again. It took me years of knowing about ETFs before I bought my first share. That early win made me realize how easy it was to buy them and gave me the confidence to continue.

Get Started Now

You need to start. Take some small step forward. Design a system you can begin so you can track your progress and stick with your plan. Keep in mind that if you grow your money you'll have more options and freedom to do what you want later in life.

You may not have $200 or $500 to start an emergency fund or Roth IRA right now. Just making ends meet can be hard for people, especially when you are young and just starting. How about $25 or $50? The key is to start saving and invest in your future as soon as you can.

I started small. I didn't even know about retirement accounts in my 20s, so I just put $100 into a mutual fund every month. That was the smartest financial decision I ever made, and eventually, I bumped it up to $200 a month. If a freelance photographer with no investment training can get an investment system off the ground you can too.

So, no matter where you are in your life, it's never too soon to start preparing for your future. And it's also never too late to get started. Don't feel like you have to do everything perfectly or get it all done at once. Small steps are all you need to take as long as you're moving forward.

If you have the desire to invest now and you don't follow through you'll probably regret it later. So, think of your future self and how happy you will be that you started now. Act today to minimize regrets.

38

HOW DO YOU DEFINE SUCCESS?

I heard a sensational podcast interview with Bill Bengen, and at the end of the episode the hosts asked him how he defines success.[1] The host ask this question of every guest, yet I don't think he expected such a deeply human and analytically rigorous response.

Since we discussed planning for success in the last chapter, I thought I'd share Bengen's definition of success because it is both simple and powerful.

I believe this wisdom deserves to be shared with the world. If one reader finds some inspiration from his definition of success, the greater chance his ideas will spread.

Podcast host Cameron Passmore asked Bengen, "How do you define success in your life?"

"Before I go to bed each night," Bengan said, "I ask myself three questions."

1. "Today, did I learn anything, or did I create something?"
2. "Did I do anything to help anybody — particularly people I love, but even for a stranger, maybe helping an old lady across the street or, you know, helping a child understand a math problem?"

3. "Have I given proper attention, you know, to this mystery and wonder of the world and the universe and being alive and being able to experience all this?"

"If I can answer 'yes' to all those questions during the day, I felt I've had a successful day," he said. "And if I look back over a period of years and think about all those days, if I felt the preponderance of those days were a success—that I checked the box, three spaces those days — I felt my life was a success."

The podcast's other host, Ben Felix said, "Bill, you know that that answer to the success question is probably the most analytically rigorous answer that we've gotten: ask three questions every day and aggregate the data over time!"

I also admire Bengan's creative, quantitive, and generous approach to life.

39

USEFUL RESOURCES

Portfolio Visualizer - https://www.portfoliovisualizer.com/ This is a valuable tool that lets users create portfolios and see how they behave under different time frames. I find the "backtest portfolio" feature to be the most useful. It allows you to see how different ETFs, stocks or mutual funds perform over different time frames.

ETFdb - etfdb.com - This website provides a ton of useful data on each ETF. They also offer tools like an ETF screener and a head-to-head comparison tool.

The Rational Reminder Podcast: The Rational Reminder Podcast serves as "a weekly reality check on sensible investing and financial decision making for Canadians." Hosted by Benjamin Felix and Cameron Passmore, each podcast focuses on a different investing topic and the podcasts often feature interviews with influential figures in the investing world. Though the podcast is intended for Canadians, I believe the concepts apply to investors worldwide. The ideas and interviews are useful for investors in any country. I particularly enjoyed two episodes, #71 relates to ETF investing and #137 is about retirement planning but provides a lot of useful tips for developing good financial practices, budgeting, and saving for retirement.

Episode 71: Guest Dave Nadig: Everything you could ever know about ETFs

Episode 135 William Bengen: The 5% Rule for Retirement Spending

THANK YOU

Art by Edwin Yaguar Chávez

Thanks for taking the time to read this book!

If you enjoyed this book and feel it would be helpful to other readers, please write a review on "The ETF Investor" page on Amazon. It will help me out a lot, thank you.

I welcome your ideas and feedback on any way I can improve this book, so please don't hesitate to share.

I appreciate your taking the time to leave a review, and I know future readers will too.

Thank you for reading,

Jeff Luke

AFTERWORD

It's hard to be all things to every reader, but I hope that you found something useful in this book regardless of what you already knew about ETFs.

No book lives in a vacuum, and this book was born at the start of the Coronavirus pandemic. My desire to take a deep dive into learning about ETFs coincided with wild stock market gyrations unlike any in history. I put ETFs to the test as a way to act decisively even when I didn't know exactly which stocks to buy, and I found they made my investment decisions simple so I could buy as the market declined without having to roll up my sleeves and try to pick individual stocks.

The world of stock and ETF investing changed in a major way in the months before the pandemic when suddenly large brokerage firms began offering commission-free trades. A large source of investor transaction costs suddenly disappeared.

I've noticed many millennials, zoomers[1], and other young investors on platforms like *Reddit, TikTok,* and *YouTube* talking about stock trades at all hours of the day and night. Investing (or gambling on "stonks[2]" as made popular by the subreddit *"Wall Street Bets"*) is not just something in the domain of old people with subscriptions to *The Wall Street Journal*. It's the wild west for everyone with a thumb, a smartphone, and a desire to get rich quickly.

As soon as I first invested with ETFs I could tell they were *really easy to use*. "Is that it?" I wondered as soon as I clicked "submit" and placed my trade. It was incredibly easy to place a trade and own this whole bunch of stocks. No going on the laptop and clicking through a bunch of windows, and no waiting to find out about the purchase price at the end of the day. In the time it takes you to read this paragraph you could have placed an order and bought an ETF. I see so many exciting things happening in the investing world it's exciting to see what will appear next.

We're already seeing new products like "fractional shares" and "direct indexing" available through brokerages like Fidelity, Robinhood, and Schwab. There have never been more options available to investors at all levels of experience.

I think one of the most exciting aspects of investing today is that with commission-free trades, anyone can design their portfolio without the help of a stockbroker, financial adviser, or mutual fund manager. From what I've seen on YouTube and many other social media platforms, many investors are rising to the challenge and creating their investment portfolios by themselves.

I think the only question that self-serve investors will have in the future is figuring out if they can get better returns buying individual stocks using commission-free trades, or if they'd get better results using an ETF. For the low-expense index ETFs this is an easy decision because the fees are so low, but once an expense ratio exceeds .50% or .75% an investor has to decide if the fund manager provides excess returns that are worth the high fee.

Since writing this book is my maiden voyage into new ETF territory there may have been some areas that I missed, barely touched upon, or omitted entirely from these pages. I hope readers will feel free to connect with me (contact info on the next page) to share any ideas or questions so I can improve the content for future readers.

Wherever you are right now on your journey I hope you found this book was fun to read, that you know more now than when you started reading, and that it has inspired you and given you the confidence to invest.

DISCLOSURE

At the time of publication the author owns the following securities mentioned in this book[1]:

- Vanguard Small Company ETF (VB)
- Vanguard S&P 500 ETF (VOO)
- Amazon.com
- Berkshire Hathaway

CONNECT

If there's anything you wish you could learn about ETFs but didn't find in these pages, please send me an email and I'll try to include the material in a future edition.

You can reach me by email at jlukephoto@gmail.com

Thanks for taking the time to read this book. I appreciate your time and look forward to hearing from you.

ABOUT THE AUTHOR

Jeff Luke lives and works as a photographer and writer in Seattle, Washington. His photography has appeared in *The New York Times* and other publications worldwide.

The ETF Investor is his fifth book about investing. Earlier titles include *Winvesting* (2020), *Smart Stocks* (2019), and *Stock Market Intelligence* (2018).

His book "Animal Donut: Images & Stories" features artistic photos of animals & donuts, and you can check them out on his website: animaldonut.com and Instagram @animaldonut

He enjoys biking, photography, writing, and taking the huskies Maximus, Snowy, and Zeus for walks along Lake Washington.

If you have any questions or would like to connect, please email jlukephoto@gmail.com

ALSO BY JEFF LUKE

Stock Market Intelligence (2018)

This was my first major book about picking stocks. It introduced the PALMS investing system to help people just starting out figure out the five questions to ask before buying any stock.

Smart Stocks (2019)

This book expands on the PALMS investing system introduced in my first book, and it dives into how to read annual reports and invest in stocks of small companies.

Winvesting (2020)

This book teaches you how to get started investing with index funds. This is an excellent book if you're a beginning investor and want to learn about index funds and how to set up your own account.

NOTES

2. What is an ETF?

1. Source: Wikipedia https://en.m.wikipedia.org/wiki/Exchange-traded_fund
2. Like mutual funds, ETFs offer investors a way to pool their money in a fund that makes investments in stocks, bonds, or other assets and, in return, to receive an interest in that investment pool. Unlike mutual funds, however, ETF shares are traded on a national stock exchange and at market prices that may or may not be the same as the net asset value ("NAV") of the shares, that is, the value of the ETF's assets minus its liabilities divided by the number of shares outstanding. Source: SEC website https://www.investor.gov/introduction-investing/investing-basics/investment-products/mutual-funds-and-exchange-traded-2
3. Source: SEC.gov https://www.investor.gov/introduction-investing/investing-basics/investment-products/mutual-funds-and-exchange-traded-2
4. Description of "Types of ETFs" from SEC website: https://www.investor.gov/introduction-investing/investing-basics/investment-products/mutual-funds-and-exchange-traded-2 Description of Ark Fintech Innovation ETF from Ark Funds website: https://ark-funds.com/fintech-etf

3. Investing made simple

1. Online trade costs disappeared when most online brokers began to offer "commission-free" trades in 2019. Source: Investor Junkie https://investorjunkie.com/stock-brokers/commission-free-brokers/
2. *Shoshin* (初心) is a word from Zen Buddhism meaning "beginner's mind." It refers to having an attitude of openness, eagerness, and lack of preconceptions when studying a subject, even when studying at an advanced level, just as a beginner would. Source: Wikipedia https://en.wikipedia.org/wiki/Shoshin
3. I don't mean to throw shade on index funds, which are a subset of mutual funds. The first index funds existed before ETFs, and they allow investors to invest in a diversified portfolio at low cost. They are formed by groups of investors who "pool" their investments and were available for purchase or sale at the end of the trading day.

    Later in this book we will investigate the differences between mutual fund and ETF structure, but for now just keep in mind that with the advent of ETFs, index funds can be traded like stocks during the day while the stock market is open.

    An index fund is a type of mutual fund or exchange traded fund (ETF) with a portfolio constructed to match or track the components of a financial market

Notes

index, such as the Standard and Poor Index (S&P 500). An index mutual fund is said to provide broad market exposure, low operating expenses, and low portfolio turnover. These funds follow their benchmark index regardless of the state of the markets. Source: Investopedia https://www.investopedia.com/terms/i/indexfund.asp

4. Ben Felix brought up this possibility during The Rational Reminder Podcast, which serves as "a weekly reality check on sensible investing and financial decision making for Canadians." Hosted by Felix and Cameron Passmore, each podcast focuses on a different investing topic and the podcasts often feature interviews with influential figures in the investing world. The question about exiting and then buying back into the market was raised by Felix during Episode 100: "Expect the Unexpected," which features a superb interview with professor Ken French.
5. "I Sold All My Stocks" by YouTuber "Beat the Bush." Source: YouTube https://www.youtube.com/watch?v=pnBQnYcIrMA&t=313s
6. "The Billionaire Interview That Tanked The Stock Market" Source: Forbes https://www.forbes.com/sites/antoinegara/2020/03/18/the-billionaire-interview-that-tanked-the-stock-market/?sh=36eeabe05b45
7. "Warren Buffett says Berkshire sold all its airline stocks because of the coronavirus" Source: CNBC https://www.cnbc.com/2020/05/02/warren-buffett-says-berkshire-sold-its-entire-position-in-airlines-because-of-the-coronavirus.html
8. When I say I owned a "slice," I refer to the legal ownership an investor becomes when they buy an ETF. Stock ownership is partial ownership of a company. In March of of 2020 Tesla was not yet a member of the S&P 500 index, but it is as of March 2021. The author purchased shares of the Vanguard S&P 500 ETF (VOO). The number of Stocks in Vanguard S&P 500 index ETF is 509 as of April 15, 2021. Source: Vanguard's website: https://investor.vanguard.com/etf/profile/portfolio/voo
9. The author purchased shares of both Vanguard S&P 500 ETF (VOO) and Vanguard Small Cap Value ETF (VB). The number of Stocks in Vanguard S&P 500 index ETF is 509 as of April 15, 2021. Source: Vanguard's website: https://investor.vanguard.com/etf/profile/portfolio/voo The number of Stocks in Vanguard Small-Cap ETF (VB) is 1442 as of April 15, 2021. Source: Vanguard's website: https://investor.vanguard.com/etf/profile/portfolio/vb
10. This is not an official name or anything, but I think it captures the short, terrifying dip in stock prices that happened during the month of March and I'm going to use it because it seems to be a fitting descriptor and better than "Covid Crash" or "March Mayhem" so I'm sticking with it.

4. Set up a brokerage account

1. A rich source of information for ETF investors is located on the SEC website, investor.gov https://www.investor.gov/introduction-investing/investing-basics/investment-products/mutual-funds-and-exchange-traded-2

Notes

5. Types of orders

1. Source: SEC website. https://www.sec.gov/fast-answers/answerstradexhtm.html
2. Source: https://www.investor.gov/introduction-investing/investing-basics/how-stock-markets-work/types-orders
3. Source: Types of Orders — SEC website. https://www.investor.gov/introduction-investing/investing-basics/how-stock-markets-work/types-orders

6. Investing at intervals

1. Daniel Kahneman changed the way we think about thinking. But what do other thinkers think of him? Source: The Guardian https://www.theguardian.com/science/2014/feb/16/daniel-kahneman-thinking-fast-and-slow-tributes
2. I have a carabiner even though I'm not a climber. I find it to be an excellent keychain. A carabiner or karabiner is a specialized type of shackle, a metal loop with a spring-loaded gate[2] used to quickly and reversibly connect components, most notably in safety-critical systems. The word is a shortened form of Karabinerhaken (or also short Karabiner), a German phrase for a "spring hook" used by a carbine rifleman, or carabinier, to attach his carabin to a belt or bandolier. Source: Wikipedia.

7. Simplicity with one ETF

1. The company data are from the Vanguard website as of Holding as of 2/29/2020. Source: Vanguard. Note that as share prices change so does the percentage of each holding in the portfolio. This Vanguard web page displays the holdings for VOO: https://investor.vanguard.com/etf/profile/VOO
2. CAGR stands for "Compound Annual Growth Rate" and represents the average rate of return for an investment. This number makes it easy to compare similar investments.
3. The words mid-cap and small-cap refer to the size, or "capitalization" of the companies held in the ETF. The capitalization is calculated by multiplying the number of shares outstanding by the share price.
4. Graph as of April 9, 2020. Source: Portfolio Visualizer. The data is only for five years because the inception date for SPDR MSCI World StrategicFactors ETF (QWLD) was June 4, 2014.
5. Active fund managers trail the S&P 500 for the ninth year in a row in triumph for indexing. Source: CNBC https://www.cnbc.com/2019/03/15/active-fund-managers-trail-the-sp-500-for-the-ninth-year-in-a-row-in-triumph-for-indexing.html
6. "Warren Buffett says he can't beat the S&P 500" Source: CNN Markets Now: https://www.cnn.com/2019/02/25/investing/warren-buffett-sp-500-stocks/index.html

Notes

8. ETFs help you keep calm

1. Source: Wikipedia https://en.wikipedia.org/wiki/Fight_Club
2. The Rational Reminder Podcast is "A weekly reality-check on sensible investing and financial decision-making for Canadians. The podcast is hosted by Benjamin Felix and Cameron Passmore, and while it is intended for Canadians, the content and ideas are excellent and apply to all investors. Professor Kenneth French appeared on Episode 200 "Expect the Unexpected." French is a professor of finance at Dartmouth and he is most famous for his work on asset pricing with Eugene Fama. They have written many academic papers, including papers that describe two factors above and beyond a stock's market beta which can explain differences in stock returns: market capitalization and "value". They also offer evidence that a variety of patterns in average returns, often labeled as "anomalies" in past work, can be explained with their Fama-French three-factor model. In 2014 Fama and French published "A Five-Factor Asset Pricing Model" which described a five-factor model directed at capturing the size, value, profitability, and investment patterns in average stock return. They found that this five-factor model performs better than their previous three-factor model.

    A bear market is a general decline in the stock market. Source: Wikipedia https://en.wikipedia.org/wiki/Market_trend

9. Factor Investing

1. Alpha (α) is a term used in investing to describe an investment strategy's ability to beat the market, or it's "edge." Alpha is thus also often referred to as "excess return" or "abnormal rate of return," which refers to the idea that markets are efficient, and so there is no way to systematically earn returns that exceed the broad market as a whole. Alpha is often used in conjunction with beta (the Greek letter β), which measures the broad market's overall volatility or risk, known as systematic market risk. Source: Investopedia "What is Alpha" https://www.investopedia.com/terms/a/alpha.asp
2. A Five-Factor Asset Pricing Model https://papers.ssrn.com/sol3/papers.cfm?abstract_id=2287202
3. "What's past is prologue" is a quotation by William Shakespeare from his play *The Tempest*. The phrase was originally used in *The Tempest*, Act 2, Scene I. Antonio uses it to suggest that all that has happened before that time, the "past", has led Sebastian and himself to this opportunity to do what they are about to do: commit murder, or make another choice. Source: Wikipedia https://en.wikipedia.org/wiki/What's_past_is_prologue
4. Bitcoin price has increased in value 14,570.50% in the past five years as of 4/16/2021 according to the Robinhood app.
5. Tesla 5-year price appreciation as of April 16, 2021 according to Robinhood app.
6. The Rational Reminder Podcast serves as "a weekly reality check on sensible investing and financial decision making for Canadians." Hosted by Benjamin

Felix and Cameron Passmore, each podcast focuses on a different investing topic and the podcasts often feature interviews with influential figures in the investing world.
7. Eugene Fama and Kenneth French's landmark paper about factor investing, "A Five-Factor Asset Pricing Model" https://papers.ssrn.com/sol3/papers.cfm?abstract_id=2287202

10. The 25 ETFs

1. Disclosure: The author owns shares of Vanguard Small-Cap ETF (VB) and Vanguard S&P 500 ETF (VOO) as of April 30, 2021.

11. Small-cap ETFs

1. You can find the number of shares outstanding through a Google search. For example, a quick search for Zoom Video Communications shows that the company has a total of 281.95 million shares outstanding. The closing price on 5/15/2020 was $174.83. If you multiply (281,950,000 x $174.83 = $49,293,318,500) which is the total market capitalization of Zoom — what the market judges the total price would be for the company if all shares were purchased at the market price. In financial shorthand, we can say Zoom has a "market cap of $49.3 billion." Small-cap companies have market caps between $300 million and $2 billion in market capitalization, so Zoom is too large to be a small-cap stock. At the time of this writing, Zoom is considered a large-cap stock. Make sure you obtain the correct number of outstanding shares for your calculation. In the example above, Zoom has a total of 281.95 million shares outstanding. This figure includes shares that are owned by company founders or insiders and these shares are not available for trading on the stock market. You will also see Zoom shares outstanding listed as 167.56 million, and this number designates shares available to trade on the market, also known as the "float." Make sure to use the first number — the total shares outstanding to get the correct market capitalization when doing your calculation. Examples of these share statistics for Zoom can be found at this link: https://seekingalpha.com/symbol/ZM/overview
2. The terms "large-cap," "mid-cap," and "small-cap" are just abbreviations for the size of the company a fund holds. The "cap" part stands for capitalization, which is calculated by multiplying the number of shares outstanding by the share price. You can find the number of shares outstanding through a simple Google search. For example, a quick search for Zoom Video Communications shows that the company has 281.95 million shares outstanding. The closing price for Zoom on 5/15/2020 was $174.83. If you multiply (281,950,000 x $174.83 = $49,293,318,500) which is the market capitalization of Zoom. We say Zoom has a market cap of $49.3 billion. Small-cap companies have between $300 million and $2 billion in market capitalization, so Zoom is too large to be

Notes

considered a small-cap stock. At the time of this writing Zoom is a large-cap stock. Source: Investopedia https://www.investopedia.com/terms/s/small-cap.asp

3. The market capitalization of these large-cap companies is based on Yahoo Finance data on May 4, 2021,
4. The fund holding information was accurate as of May 7, 2020, as listed on etfdb.com unless noted otherwise. If you want updated information please search that database or do an online search for the ETF in question to get more current data on fund holdings, returns, etc.
5. Source: iShares Core S&P Small-Cap ETF (IJR) fact sheet: https://www.ishares.com/us/literature/fact-sheet/ijr-ishares-core-s-p-small-cap-etf-fund-fact-sheet-en-us.pdf
6. Schwab US Small-Cap ETF fact sheet. Source: Schwab website: https://www.schwab.com/public/schwab/investing/investment_help/investment_research/etf_research/etfs.html?path=/Prospect/Research/etfs/summary.asp%3Fsymbol%3DSCHA
7. As of May 8, 2020. Source: ETFdb.com
8. According to etfdb.com as of 5/7/2020.
9. https://www.spglobal.com/spdji/en/indices/equity/sp-600/#data
10. CRSP is an acronym for Center for Research in Security Prices. Since 1960, CRSP has provided research-quality data to scholarly researchers and advanced the body of knowledge in finance, economics and related disciplines. Today, nearly 500 leading academic institutions in 35 countries rely on CRSP data for academic research and to support classroom instructions.

    Investment practitioners rely on CRSP data to backtest strategies and to benchmark investment performance. Source: CRSP website: http://www.crsp.org/about-crsp
11. Source: CRSP Indexes http://www.crsp.org/files/crspsc1_quarterly_report-march2021.pdf
12. Comparison of IJR and VB made using the "Head-to-Head" ETF comparison tool on ETFdb.com. Data as of April 29, 2021. https://etfdb.com/tool/etf-comparison/IJR-VB%20/#performance
13. The Rational Reminder Podcast serves as "a weekly reality check on sensible investing and financial decision making for Canadians." Hosted by Benjamin Felix and Cameron Passmore, each podcast focuses on a different investing topic and the podcasts often feature interviews with influential figures in the investing world. I greatly enjoyed episode 135 of the Rational Reminder Podcast with guest William Bengen "The 5% Rule for Retirement Spending." Bengen was an upbeat, intelligent guest with more than 30 years of experience on his side, and he presented his findings in a way that was both factually rich and easy to understand.
14. Source: Amazon author page. https://www.amazon.com/William-P.-Bengen/e/B001HPGOL6%3Fref=dbs_a_mng_rwt_scns_share
15. Bengen's 1994 paper, "Determining Withdrawal Rates Using Historical Data" explained that retirees could withdraw 4% of their investment portfolio annually. In December of 2020 he updated his findings after years of research to

reveal that high stock prices, coupled with low inflation expectations, increase the expected withdrawal rate to 4.5% or more. He said the initial 4% figure was actually the "worst-case scenario" and since writing his initial paper he has changed his withdrawal rate protections. Bengen said today's economic environment is different from the late 1960s or early 1970s, and people can be more optimistic now. Bengen said the average investor could withdraw 7% or more, with "a couple lucky investors" able to withdraw a maximum of 13% a year.

16. The concept is that diversifying assets provides a useful benefit at little to no extra cost. Investors who buy only one asset-class, or only large-cap stocks may be utilizing a small part of the available investment universe. The topic of how many different asset classes and how widely diversified a portfolio should be is a source of endless debate. Some investors believe one total stock market fund or S&P 500 index fund provide amble diversification, while others believe an investor should invest in small-cap, large-cap, international, and bond ETFs. There is an endless supply of opinions on how many investments are "enough," and it's up to each investor to find the combination that works for them. Source of Markowitz quote: Forbes Books https://forbesbooks.com/diversification-is-the-only-free-lunch/

12. Small-cap Value ETFs

1. Source: Investopedia https://www.investopedia.com/top-10-s-and-p-500-stocks-by-index-weight-4843111
2. Source: "A Five-Factor Asset Pricing Model" by Eugene Fama and Kenneth French https://papers.ssrn.com/sol3/papers.cfm?abstract_id=2287202
3. Portfolio Visualizer - https://www.portfoliovisualizer.com/ This tool provides a free tool for investors to create hypothetical portfolios that show how different assets behave during different periods. I find the "backtest portfolio" feature to be the most useful. It allows you to do "head-to-head" comparisons of ETFs, stocks, and mutual funds to see relative performance over time.
4. A bid-ask spread is the amount by which the ask price exceeds the bid price for an asset in the market. The bid-ask spread is essentially the difference between the highest price that a buyer is willing to pay for an asset and the lowest price that a seller is willing to accept. An individual looking to sell will receive the bid price while one looking to buy will pay the ask price. The market makers who join buyers and sellers typically profit from the "spread" and sometimes share this profit with the stock brokerage firms that provide them with order flow. Source: Investopedia https://www.investopedia.com/terms/b/bid-askspread.asp
5. Source: Morningstar ETF Investor Report.
6. Source: Avantis website https://www.avantisinvestors.com/content/avantis/en/investments/avantis-u-s-small-cap-value-etf.html
7. Source: Bridgeway Funds website: https://bridgewayfunds.com/mutual-funds/omni-mutual-funds/ultra-small-company-market/
8. Source: RWJ Overview on ETF Database https://www.etf.com/RWJ#overview

Notes

9. Source: RWJ Overview on ETF Database https://www.etf.com/RWJ#overview
10. Source: Morningstar ETF report April 29, 2021.
11. Morningstar ETF report as of April 30, 2021 Source: https://www.morningstar.com/etfs/arcx/rwj/performance

13. Mega-Cap Growth ETF

1. As of May 7, 2020. Source: ETFdb.com
2. Source: etfdb.com as of 5/7/2020
3. Source: Marketwatch.com 5/7/2020 https://www.marketwatch.com/investing/index/spx
4. As of May 7, 2020. Source: ETFdb.com

14. Mid-cap ETFs

1. "What is Mid-Cap?" Source: Investopedia https://www.investopedia.com/terms/m/midcapstock.asp
2. As of May 27, 2021. Source: ETFdb.com. This ETF's ticker symbol has been updated from JKH to IMCG to reflect the ETF company's change since this book's first edition. This ETF's expense ratio decreased from .30% to .06% since the first edition. Note that the largest position in this fund, Moderna (MRNA) was not listed in the top 15 stock holdings a year earlier, a reflection of Moderna's rapid growth, and also a characteristic of many fast-growing mid-cap stocks.
3. As of May 27, 2021. Source: ETFdb.com
4. As of May 27, 2021. Source: ETFdb.com
5. "After 150 days of the COVID-19 pandemic, here are the best- and worst-performing stocks" Source: Marketwatch https://www.marketwatch.com/story/after-150-days-of-the-covid-19-pandemic-here-are-the-best--and-worst-performing-stocks-2020-08-10
6. "After 150 days of the COVID-19 pandemic, here are the best- and worst-performing stocks" Source: Marketwatch https://www.marketwatch.com/story/after-150-days-of-the-covid-19-pandemic-here-are-the-best--and-worst-performing-stocks-2020-08-10
7. Source: Wikipedia https://en.wikipedia.org/wiki/Horace
8. The 1-year return data is for the period from May 27, 2020 through May 27, 2021.

15. VanEck Vectors Morningstar Wide Moat

1. As of April 8, 2020. Source: ETFdb.com
2. As of April 8th, 2020. Source: Morningstar Investment Research Center
3. As of April 8, 2020. Source: ETFdb.com

16. O'Shares Global Internet Giants

1. Source: O'Shares website: https://oshares.com/ogig/
2. As of May 7, 2020. Source: ETFdb.com
3. Source: Morningstar Research Center. May 14, 2020.
4. Source: Ark Website as of 6/12/2020 ARKW Holdings: https://ark-funds.com/wp-content/fundsiteliterature/holdings/ARK_NEXT_GENERATION_INTERNET_ETF_ARKW_HOLDINGS.pdf

17. ARK Innovation

1. Source: ARK funds website: ark-funds.com
2. Source: Ark Invest website. Source: https://ark-invest.com/
3. Source: ETFdb as of June 2, 2020 https://etfdb.com/etf/ARKK/#holdings
4. Source: Ark funds website as of June 12, 2020

18. WisdomTree Cloud Computing

1. Source: Wisdom Tree website: www.wisdomtree.com/etfs/thematic/wcld
2. YTD information for WCLD and S&P 500 as of June 12, 2020. Source: Morningstar
3. As of May 7, 2020. Source: ETFdb.com
4. As of May 7, 2020. Source: ETFdb.com

19. SPDR S&P Biotech

1. Data from etfdb.com as of May 7, 2020

20. iShares Nasdaq Biotechnology

1. Data from etfdb.com as of May 7, 2020
2. CAGR stands for "Compound Annual Growth Rate" and represents the average rate of return for an investment. This number makes it easy to compare similar investments.

21. Vanguard Health Care

1. Data from etfdb.com as of May 7, 2020

Notes

22. Three Dividend ETFs

1. Understanding Dividend Yield. Source: The Balance https://www.thebalance.com/understanding-dividend-yield-3140782
2. For consistency the dividend yield data is as reflected on etfdb.com as of 5/7/2020. This data will likely change over time.

23. Blackrock iShares Core Dividend Growth

1. Data from etfdb.com as of May 7, 2020
2. Source: iShares website https://www.ishares.com/us/products/264623/ishares-core-dividend-growth-etf
3. Data from etfdb.com as of May 7, 2020

24. ProShares S&P 500 Dividend Aristocrats fund

1. Data from etfdb.com as of May 7, 2020
2. The fund's website describes this ETF as "focusing exclusively on the S&P 500 Dividend Aristocrats—high-quality companies that have not just paid dividends but grown them for at least 25 consecutive years, with most doing so for 40 years or more." Source - Proshares website: https://www.proshares.com/funds/nobl.html
3. Data from etfdb.com as of May 7, 2020

25. Global X Super Dividend Fund

1. Data from etfdb.com as of May 7, 2020
2. "The Rational Reminder" podcast is described as "A weekly reality-check on sensible investing and financial decision-making for Canadians." It's hosted by Benjamin Felix and Cameron Passmore of PWL Capital. I first discovered Ben Felix on his YouTube channel where I discovered mention of the podcast. David Nadig was a guest on November 7, 2019, and Episode 71 is titled "Everything that you could ever know about ETFs with David Nadig." Nadig knows his stuff, and The Rational Reminder was a sensational forum for his discussion of ETF investing. rationalreminder.ca/podcast/ep-71
3. Data from etfdb.com as of May 7, 2020

26. Ark Fintech Innovation

1. Source: Merriam-Webster
2. Source: Ark Funds website: https://ark-funds.com/fintech-etf

Notes

3. Source: Ark website - list of Ark Fintech Innovation holdings as of June 12, 2020.
4. Data from etfdb.com as of June 12, 2020
5. Ark Fintech Innovation has an inception date of Feb 01, 2019. 1-Year and YTD performance figures are as of June 12, 2020. Source: Morningstar.

27. Technology Sector ETFs

1. Data from etfdb.com as of May 7, 2020
2. Data from etfdb.com as of May 7, 2020
3. Data from etfdb.com as of May 7, 2020
4. Source: Invesco https://www.invesco.com/us/financial-products/etfs/product-detail?productId=qqq
5. Source: All data for three funds below from etfdb.com 5/7/2020
6. CAGR stands for "Compound Annual Growth Rate" and represents the average rate of return for an investment. This number makes it easy to compare similar investments.

28. International ETFs

1. Data from etfdb.com as of May 7, 2020
2. Data from etfdb.com as of May 7, 2020
3. CAGR stands for "Compound Annual Growth Rate" and represents the average rate of return for an investment. This number makes it easy to compare similar investments.
4. The graph and performance data cover the time from 2012-2020 because VXUS was established in 2011. The fund's emerging markets exposure has caused the fund's returns to lag those of VEA by a small margin due to developing markets underperforming developed markets during this period.
5. "Developing" and "emerging" markets are used synonymously. Both terms refer to companies in countries that are not considered to possess the economic stability of "developed" market economies. VEA invests only in developed markets, while VXUS invests approximately 75% of its assets in developed markets and 25% of its assets in "developing" or "emerging markets." Source: Vanguard website as of 3/31/2020. https://investor.vanguard.com/etf/profile/VXUS

29. Putting it all together

1. "Small-Cap Withdrawal Magic" Source: Financial Advisor Magazine https://www.fa-mag.com/news/small-cap-withdrawal-magic-28553.html
2. The Rational Reminder Podcast serves as "a weekly reality check on sensible investing and financial decision making for Canadians." Hosted by Benjamin

Notes

Felix and Cameron Passmore, each podcast focuses on a different investing topic and the podcasts often feature interviews with influential figures in the investing world. I greatly enjoyed episode 135 of the Rational Reminder Podcast with guest William Bengen titled, "The 5% Rule for Retirement Spending." Bengen was an upbeat, intelligent guest who brought more than 30 years of retirement investing experience to the podcast. He presented his findings with well-researched data and a sense of humor that conveyed a message that was factually rich and easy to grasp.

3. "Diversification Is the Only Free Lunch," by Benjamin C. Halliburton. Source: Forbes Books https://forbesbooks.com/diversification-is-the-only-free-lunch/

30. Your biggest obstacle

1. Fractional shares let investors purchase ETF shares or stock based on a dollar amount they select rather than the price of a whole share. "Fractional Shares: What They Are and Where to Buy Them" Source: Nerd Wallet https://www.nerdwallet.com/article/investing/fractional-shares
2. 58% of Americans Have Less Than $1,000 in Savings, Survey Finds. Source: Yahoo Financehttps://finance.yahoo.com/news/58-americans-less-1-000-090000503.html
3. Richard Thaler Interview, "Richard Thaler Interview: the less attention you pay, the more money you'll have" Source: YouTube

31. Active managers choose index investing

1. "When investors make mistakes, and they always do, this manager pounces and profits" Source: Marketwatch https://www.marketwatch.com/story/when-investors-make-mistakes-and-they-always-do-this-manager-pounces-and-profits-2019-02-26
2. Source: Fuller & Thaler https://www.fullerthaler.com/
3. Richard Thaler Interview: "the less attention you pay, the more money you'll have." Source: YouTube. Fuller & Thaler Asset Management, Inc. offers actively managed mutual funds.
4. An index fund is a pooled investment that you purchase through a broker or directly from a mutual fund company. For example, the Vanguard S&P 500 index fund (VFIAX). The same stocks can also be purchased on an exchange using an ETF (Voo). The stocks in the portfolio are the same, but the investment vehicle is different.

Notes

33. A behavior trick

1. "8 Brilliant Lessons From The Investor That Taught Warren Buffett Everything He Knows" Source: Business Insider.

34. Pay yourself first

1. YouTube channel: Investing With Rose
2. Source: YouTube — Budgeting For Beginners - 8 Places Your Money Needs to Go: https://youtu.be/FGEsWFj8fl8
3. $6,000 a year is the limit for people under 50 years old as of 2020. For those over 50 years old, the limit is $7,000 a year.

35. Think About Rip Van Winkle

1. Richard Thaler Interview: The less attention you pay, the more money you'll have" Source: YouTube

36. Creation and redemption

1. "The Rational Reminder" podcast is "A weekly reality check on sensible investing and financial decision-making for Canadians." It's hosted by Benjamin Felix and Cameron Passmore of PWL Capital. I first discovered Ben Felix on his YouTube channel where I discovered mention of the podcast. David Nadig was a guest on November 7, 2019 and Episode 71 is titled "Everything that you could ever know about ETFs with David Nadig." Nadig knows his stuff, and The Rational Reminder was a sensational forum for his discussion of ETF investing. rationalreminder.ca/podcast/ep-71
2. ETF Creation & Redemption. Source: YouTube https://www.youtube.com/watch?v=2-Voq-ivplg&t=690s
3. I discovered David Nadig when he was a guest on "The Rational Reminder" podcast, which is hosted by Benjamin Felix and Cameron Passmore of PWL Capital. Nadig was a guest on November 7, 2019 and Episode 71 is titled "Everything that you could ever know about ETFs with David Nadig" and it is aptly named. He explained creation and redemption, direct indexing, and optimized vs. full replication methods of ETF design. Nadig clearly knows his stuff.
4. This detailed information about creation and redemption is based on clear explanations of the process by David Nadig, who was a guest on Episode 71 of "The Rational Reminder" podcast. Additionally, he explains the mechanism in a YouTube video titled "ETF Creation & Redemption."
5. "ETF Creation & Redemption" on the ETF.com YouTube channel. Excellent explanation of ETF Creation and Redemption by David Nadig. https://www.

203

Notes

youtube.com/watch?v=2-Voq-ivplg&t=690s
6. ETF Creation & Redemption video: Source: YouTube https://youtu.be/2-Voq-ivplg

37. Plan for success

1. 59 Seconds: Change Your Life in Under a Minute by Richard Wiseman. Anchor Books, 2009.

38. How do you define success?

1. The Rational Reminder Podcast serves as "a weekly reality check on sensible investing and financial decision making for Canadians." Hosted by Benjamin Felix and Cameron Passmore, each podcast focuses on a different investing topic and the podcasts often feature interviews with influential figures in the investing world. I greatly enjoyed episode 135 of the Rational Reminder Podcast with guest William Bengen "The 5% Rule for Retirement Spending." Bengen was an upbeat, intelligent guest with more than 30 years of experience on his side, and he presented his findings in a way that was both factually rich and easy to understand.

Afterword

1. *Zoomer* is a nickname referring to members of Generation Z, those born in the late 90s and early 2000s. It's a popular monicker lately as a contrast to *boomer*. Source: Merriam Webster https://www.merriam-webster.com/words-at-play/words-were-watching-zoomer-gen-z
2. In internet slang, *stonks* is a deliberate misspelling of *stocks*. It is often used as a funny way to refer to stocks, especially on message boards like Reddit's WallStreetBets and other social media sites. Source: https://www.dictionary.com/e/memes/stonks/

Disclosure

1. Holdings as of May 15, 2020.

www.ingramcontent.com/pod-product-compliance
Lightning Source LLC
Chambersburg PA
CBHW052349220526
45465CB00003BA/1030